Speech Writing for Every Occasion

How to write, present and deliver the perfect speech

A De Sales Book

Speech Writing for Every Occasion

Published 2013 by arima publishing

www.arimapublishing.com

ISBN 978 1 84549 589 3

© First De Sales Limited Partnership, 2013

A catalogue record of this book is available from the British Library

arima publishing
ASK House, Northgate Avenue
Bury St Edmunds, Suffolk IP32 6BB
t: (+44) 01284 700321

www.arimapublishing.com

Speech Writing for Every Occasion
How to write, present and deliver the perfect speech

Contents

Part Two: Wedding Speeches

Part Three: Social Occasions

Part Four: Charity Events

Introduction

Introduction

A great speech will be remembered for years, sometimes decades. A poor one will, if you're lucky, soon be forgotten. However, even disastrous speeches are sometimes unforgettable and delivering one of these could end up costing your business money or might even alienate you from friends and family.

The ability to communicate clearly and effectively is a skill that is increasingly important within our modern media dominated society. From Facebook comments and Twitter tweets to online reviews and eBay descriptions, presentation is everything. Making a speech is no different, it is merely an amplification. Whether you are speaking to business colleagues, wedding guests or to close friends, your audience will expect to be able to understand and appreciate the message that you are delivering.

Speech Writing for Every Occasion offers a simple, practical guide that will help you to prepare, write and deliver speeches and presentations at a wide range of events and venues. As well as common occasions such as wedding speeches, after dinner talks and business presentations, this book covers more off-beat or unusual applications of the speech writer's craft, including charity fund-raising events, funerals and media interviews.

The impetus behind Speech Writing for Every Occasion comes from a group of individuals who are experts in their own fields and well used to delivering keynote, business, after-dinner and motivational speeches. Frustrated by the limited scope and ambition of existing speech writing guides, they have applied their combined skill and experience to create a straightforward, pragmatic book that is packed with original tips and information.

Whether you are new to the world of speech writing or a seasoned orator, Speech Writing for Every Occasion will act as your one-stop guide. You will find yourself returning to its pages again and again in search of those nuggets of advice that separate this book on speech writing from all others.

The Bare Essentials
Speaking in Public: An Overview

- Preparation: Before You Put Pen to Paper
- Structure: Beginning, Middle and End
- Delivery: Finding Your Voice
- Aftermath: Questions and Answers

It is said that most people are more afraid of making a speech than they are of dying. This is probably an exaggeration but a fear of speaking in public does rank highly in lists of people's phobias. Fortunately it is one of those stressful events whose effects can be lessened with the application of forethought, preparation and rehearsal.

There are, of course, many different occasions where a person may be required to speak in public. It might be at a formal event, such as a conference presentation or business pitch; or it could be a social or family get together such as a wedding or anniversary party. Whatever the occasion, the principles behind assembling and delivering your speech are similar, even though the content will vary considerably.

This introductory chapter offers an overview of the mechanics behind writing and delivering a coherent speech. It should allow you to grasp the basic concepts; after this you should use the other chapters in this book to tailor your speech to the particular occasion concerned.

Preparation: before you put pen to paper

Preparation is the foundation upon which any great speech is built. If you cut corners at this stage then the results can be disastrous. Get it right and you will have the confidence to speak with authority and to deal with any tricky or unexpected situations that arise.

Remember the rule of the six Ps:
Proper Preparation and Planning Prevents Poor Performance

The precise content of your speech will have to be appropriate to the sort of occasion at which you will be speaking. The individual chapters in this book will help you with this. At this stage you should be aware of the following general tips which apply to most types of speech writing:

- Start preparing your speech well ahead of time. Do not leave it until the last minute.

- If you have been given any instructions or guidelines (e.g. the speech's title, length of speech required, what information you should or shouldn't include, etc.) then make sure you read and fully understand what you are required to do.

- Think about your audience. Ask yourself who they will be and what they will want/expect you to say. In particular, think about what could interest or offend sectors of the audience.

- Find out in advance about the venue and the facilities that will be on offer. There is no point in preparing a series of computer-generated slides if the venue does not have a digital projector.

- If using computer-generated material then make sure that it is saved in a format that can be used at the venue (e.g. find out which version of Microsoft's PowerPoint they are using). Take a copy of the file in more than one format (e.g. on a CD-ROM and a USB memory stick) so that if something goes wrong with one, you have a backup.

- Research your speech by following the advice given in the individual chapters in this book. Be wary of taking too much information from the Internet, especially facts, figures and quotes, unless you are certain that they are correct.

- Write out the speech in full then read it out loud. This will highlight any awkward sentences or difficult to pronounce words. Make adjustments as you go along until you have a speech that you can deliver fluently and confidently. Make sure that you have removed any unnecessary words such as 'very', extremely', etc.

- Consider using cue cards as an *aide mémoir* rather than reading your speech from a script. Only use bullet points written in a clear, size 16 font.

- Practice your speech as often as possible. Time yourself but remember that on the day you will probably take longer to deliver the speech than during rehearsals. Make allowance for this, e.g. if you are to speak for 30 minutes then your rehearsals should be coming in at 20 to 25 minutes.

- Write out a checklist of things that you must take with you. It is all too easy to forget important objects, such a laptop or CD-ROM, when you are nervous or getting ready in a hurry.

The structure: a beginning, middle and end

Most speeches are divided into three parts:
- A beginning
- A middle
- An end

This might seem like an obvious thing to say but it is a basic rule that is often overlooked. Understanding the role played by these three sections in structuring a speech will help you to plan what you are going to say.

The beginning

Some speeches, especially those given at weddings, already have a format for their beginning which can be followed and adapted to suit your needs. With most other types of speech the beginning section is the means by which you introduce yourself to the audience and offer them an overview of the topic on which you are about to speak.

The key with this introduction is to keep it brief and to the point while at the same time grabbing your audience's attention. This is a common technique in movies where the opening few minutes contain an action-packed sequence which immediately draws you into the plot. Some professionals call this the 'hook' because it is designed to catch an audience's attention. It is a bit like the lurid headlines on newspapers which are designed to catch your eye and make you buy a copy.

In conference situations 'the hook' is sometimes achieved by opening a talk with a shocking, intriguing or striking headline fact or image. However, an audience can be hooked in many different ways, such by telling an amusing or interesting story which relates you to the subject of your talk. For example, at a wedding anniversary many people begin by relating how they met their wife/husband. Another commonly tactic is to pose a polemical question that you then spend the rest of the talk explaining.

In most circumstances you should use the beginning to tell the audience who you are, what you are talking about and why you are qualified to speak on this subject. You should achieve this in no more than a couple of minutes.

The middle

The middle part of a speech should take up the bulk of your time on stage. It is in this section that you will be talking at length on your chosen topic. Because of this the middle section should be logically structured so that an audience can follow it easily.

It sometimes helps to decide upon the fact, theme or anecdote with which you wish to finish your speech and then think about the steps that you need to take in order to get from the beginning of your speech to this point. If you have several points or stories which you wish to relate then try writing these on individual postcards or Post-it notes and then arranging and re-arranging until you find a structure that you are happy with.

In the case of a wedding speech this could mean organising the anecdotes so that you begin with humorous recollections about the bride/groom and finish with compliments and serious observations.

When speaking about a person's life, it is usual to tell their story in chronological order: e.g. birth, education, work, etc. The same is true when talking about certain events or projects which have a point of origin, a development and a results phase.

As ever, be wary of jokes, especially those that you might find on the Internet. Unless you are an experienced stand-up comedian, getting the correct tone and emphasis for a joke is difficult. As a general guide, ask yourself the following questions before including a joke in your speech:

- Is it funny?
- Can you say it confidently or will you stumble?
- Is there any danger (however remote) of offending anyone?
- Will your audience understand and appreciate it?

Depending on the nature of your speech, the middle section is when you will want to use the most number of visual aids. It is better to use these sparingly and not to make them too cluttered. Do not include images, quotes or other superfluous information unless it is absolutely relevant to your talk.

Make sure that each slide will be visible long enough for to allow people to copy down any information on it. This is especially true if you are offering contact information, such as a telephone number, website or e-mail address.

When taking images or text from the Internet, be wary of copyright infringement. Some conferences like to make their delegates' slides available as a booklet or on a website. If your slides are to be published in print or online then please make sure that you know who owns the copyright to any images and text.

The end

The end section of your speech should be brief. Some types of speech already have a prescribed format that usually involves thanking individuals or proposing a toast: see individual chapters for details. For other speeches, the end section should be used to draw together everything you have said into a single conclusion or summary.

If the occasion is appropriate then try to leave your audience on a high. This might mean highlighting the success or future potential of a project or, at more social occasions, it might mean finding a suitable quote or finishing line which will give the audience a last laugh. Make it clear that you have finished and, if appropriate, thank any people who have helped you.

Delivery: finding your voice

The advice offered in this section is mostly common sense.

It is the prospect of delivering a speech that generates fear in most people. It is normal to be nervous before speaking in public but you can minimise this problem by being properly prepared (see the *Preparation* section above).

Bear the following things to bear in mind when you are preparing to speak:

- Dress appropriately.

- Arrive early and look around the venue. Check the seating plan, lighting, sound, etc., so that you know where you'll be speaking, where the audience will be and what facilities (such as microphones) will be available to you.

- Talk to the person who will be introducing you. Make sure that they have all the information they need and that they tell you where you will be standing and how they will be introducing you.

- Do not use a handheld microphone if you are nervous.

- Leave your notes or cards on the lectern or table. Do not hold them in your hand.

- Be sober and clear headed. Alcohol and tranquillisers will hinder, not help you.

- Before your presentation choose a moment go to the toilet. While there look in the mirror and check your appearance and clothing.

- Do not rush: speak slowly and clearly. Project your voice towards the back of the room. Do not look down and do not speak when you are faced away from your audience (e.g. when looking behind you at a slide). Try not to turn your back on the audience at all.

- Do not tell the audience you are nervous or that this is your first ever public speech.

- Look up at the audience whenever possible. Look out into the depths of the room or focus on a individual or object at the back of the room.

Aftermath: questions and answers

In most social situations, such as weddings and anniversaries, the end of your speech simply requires you to accept some applause before retaking your seat. However, if you are delivering a presentation then you may be required to accept questions from the audience.

If you expect to be questioned then make sure you know whether the venue will expect you to be in charge of picking the questioners from the audience (usually those with their hands up) or whether there will be a chairman or chairwoman who will choose for you. Similarly, find out whether a microphone will be handed to the questioner (a common practice in large auditoriums). If so, then you will need to allow time for the microphone to get to the person concerned.

Sometimes a call for questions can result in a resounding silence. This may be because of a collective shyness that can descend upon an audience, rather than a reflection of the content of your talk. You can handle this situation by preparing an obvious question of your own in advance of the talk.

If met with silence then you can fain surprise that are there no questions and then say something like: 'Well, I expected someone to ask about the...' This can break the ice and you will find that other questions will follow. If not, then at least you have made an effort and have not had to stand still in total silence for several minutes.

With formal presentations, you should consider taking business cards and/ or a one page synopsis of your talk to hand out to people that approach you after you have finished.

Hopefully this introduction will have provided you with an overview of the basic principles behind assembling and delivering a speech. You should now take advantage of the detailed chapters in this book to delve deeper into the specifics of speeches for particular occasions.

Part One
Speaking to Professionals

A Moment of Inspiration
Speaking to a Professional Audience: General Advice

It was a cold winter's day in January 1962 when a nervous-looking, young John F. Kennedy was handed a sheaf of papers containing the words of his inaugural address. It is alleged that Kennedy had just minutes to familiarise himself with his speech and yet he managed to produce a performance which is still remembered as one of the most inspirational and motivational speeches ever delivered.

Kennedy's words and delivery were perfectly suited to a world that was mired in conflict and political uncertainty. As speeches go, this one had the hallmark of greatness and it peaked when in slow and measured terms he told his fellow countrymen:

> *Ask not what your country can do for you – ask what you can do for your country.*

The new president not only inspired his fellow Americans, but galvanised the world into 'giving peace a chance'. For many that inaugural address marked the start of America's post-war era and the beginnings of a revolution in which young people gained a voice, identity and self-belief which has since come to define many aspects of the modern world.

The speech's anonymous authors created a masterpiece which, combined with Kennedy's instinctive understanding of his audience, set out a template for a new generation of motivational writers. If it is true that

John F. Kennedy had not read the speech before he stepped into the cold Washington air, then the feat is more remarkable still.

The President's words had the power to change lives. With a few simple phrases, he painted a picture of the challenges facing America and other countries. He also left people in little doubt that if they wanted to change the world, then they would have to contribute.

John F. Kennedy, of course, was not the only politician whose speeches could motive people. Sir Winston Churchill was another great orator, able to inspire through the power of spoken words. Unlike JFK, Churchill seldom used speech writers, often preferring to speak off the cuff and without the aid of any written advice.

It is reckoned that Churchill's 'Blood, Sweat and Tears' speech, made in the early summer of 1940, galvanised a browbeaten Britain to begin the long fight back against Hitler's Germany. At a time of despondence and uncertainty Churchill rallied his weary people with one of the most frequently quoted speeches of all time.

We shall defend our island whatever the cost may be. We shall fight on beaches, landing grounds, in field, in streets and on the hills. We shall never surrender and even if, which I do not for one moment believe, this island or a large part of it were subjugated and starving, them our empire beyond the seas, armed and guarded by the British Fleet, will carry on the struggle until in God's good time, the New World with all its powers and might, sets forth to the liberation and rescue of the old.

With speeches like this Churchill uplifted and mobilised an entire country and it is worth studying this particular speech if you are preparing a motivational talk of your own.

Churchill and Kennedy often used inspirational stories to enthuse and energise their audiences. Hearing an inspirational story can be a powerful tool in helping people recognise and understand the ambitions you hold for them. You are not telling a story for its own sake or for entertainment but to help achieve your goals.

There are some simple steps to remember when you set out to write a business speech or presentation. Perhaps the most important is to remember that the presentation is not about you. It is about ensuring your listeners take something positive away from the gathering and, at the same time, convincing them that they have an important part to play in the future. Below are some basic rules that will help you.

- Decide what message you want to deliver and what it is you want to achieve. This may sound obvious but it is surprising how many presentations have no clear objective. From the outset make sure your audience is aware of what your talk is about. Then make sure that your speech is tailored so that it covers all the areas required to deliver your message and nothing more. Do not be tempted to over elaborate. Keep it simple: people rarely respond well to speakers whom they think they are trying to be too clever.

- Make sure you know what is expected from you. How long should the speech be? How many people will you be addressing? Try and check out the venue ahead of time and always ask what equipment will be available. It is also very important to know about any other speakers and the areas they will be covering.

- Establish your credibility by demonstrating expertise and knowledge of the subject. Back this up with facts and statistics as well as any relevant personal experience.

- Think about how best you can present any problems or shortcomings so that they do not detract from the central message of your speech. Offer potential solutions to problems or discuss alternatives. Use your passion for a subject to convince an audience that any issues or obstacles can be surmounted. This in itself can be a useful motivational tool.

- Try to anticipate what will motivate and inspire your audience. Some audiences may respond better to a more direct and robust approach whilst others could prefer gentler coaching. Understanding an audience's needs will allow you to tailor your words in such a way that they will have much more impact.

- If possible, use stories and anecdotes to motivate the group you are addressing. This will be more memorable than an endless series of graphs, facts and figures. People respond well to stories. They help to keep an audience alert and inspired, especially if some humour is involved. Make sure your speech is not over-long.

- Try to speak with conviction and confidence. That way your audience will be more sympathetic to your message and have the confidence to follow you towards your goal. Most of us cannot pick up a speech and deliver it perfectly, as Kennedy did, but instead must rehearse and practice until the words have become like second nature.

- Computer generated slides (such as PowerPoint displays) are helpful but do not overdo it. It is better to have a few general slides that you can talk around rather than using dozens to illustrate small points. Too many slides can be confusing and will distract attention away from what you are saying. It is remarkable how often technical glitches occur - most are resolvable but some are not. Make sure you are prepared for equipment failure by having paper copies of slides.

You almost certainly will not have a behind-the-scenes team like President Kennedy so it will be up to you to turn your speech into your own creation. Practice your delivery so that you can use brief notes or cue cards as a prompt, rather than having to read from a script. The audience must be engaged, so look up regularly and make eye contact. This will make you appear sincere and help listeners to focus on your message.

It is important to keep your audience engaged and interested. This is not easy, especially if you are allocated a slot just before lunch or at the end of the day when an audience's mind may wander onto other things. A little humour will keep people's interest and do not be frightened to step up the pace of your speech, or even shorten it, if you think the audience's mood necessitates this.

Try to use your normal conversational voice and do not be tempted to introduce too much jargon or too many acronyms. This can be off-putting or even irritating. If you can display confidence and enthusiasm then you will keep an audience's interest. The last couple of minutes of your talk should be used to sum up precisely, but concisely, so that your listeners are in no doubt about your message. Do not forget to acknowledge your hosts and any others who have helped.

A good speech should elicit a response from an audience and that usually means questions. Be sure to leave an adequate amount of time to deal with these: around five to ten minutes should suffice, depending on the time available to you. If you know your material well then it should be possible to anticipate many questions so it is advisable to prepare some answers in advance.

Do not be afraid to respond to a question. If you are unable to provide an immediate answer then say so and offer to take the questioner's contact details so that you can get back to them. If possible, make yourself available after the speech so that people can speak to you on their own.

Making any speech is not easy, but if you succeed you will find the experience both rewarding and uplifting. Your goals should be to motivate and inspire others; to change people's working lives so that when you sit down, your speech delivered, your audience will be energised and inspired to chase their own dream.

The Business Presentation
Speeches for a Conference or Seminar

- Preparation: Get Your Thoughts in Order
- Writing Your Speech: Putting Flesh on the Bones
- Visual Aids: Keep it Simple
- Rehearse: Practice makes Perfect
- Delivery: Facing Your Audience
- Question and Answer Sessions
- Top Tips

How many us have sat through a mumbled speech, read verbatim from a script to a backdrop of slides that are flashed up in quick succession?

Such talks are dispiriting and tedious for an audience, many of whom will leave the auditorium with little memory or understanding of what has just been said. This is not just frustrating for conference attendees but also a lost opportunity for the speaker, whose message will have fallen upon deaf ears.

The need to assemble and deliver a presentation will affect most professional people at some point in their career. It might be an informal talk to your colleagues or it could be a full-blown group presentation to an international delegation. Either way, it is important that you deliver a talk that not only gets your message across in an intelligent and interesting fashion, but also has the ability to linger in people's minds.

Achieving this is not as difficult as it might seem but it will require you to devote a little time and thought towards the preparation and delivery of your presentation. This chapter will guide you through this process and will offer advice and techniques that should enable you to hold an audience in the palm of your hand, and keep it there.

Preparation: get your thoughts in order

By their simplest definition, conferences and seminars are formal or semi-formal occasions which are built around individual or group presentations given to an audience. Such presentations can offer a company, institution or individual the opportunity to deliver a coherent message about themselves and their ideas to people who may be potential collaborators, investors or buyers. Getting your presentation right is therefore very important.

Speaking in public is not everybody's cup of tea and receiving an invite to give a presentation can be a daunting prospect. It is natural to feel nervous or even anxious at the idea of assembling a presentation and delivering it in public. If, however, you dwell too long on the negative aspects of giving a presentation (such as having to speak in public) then you risk focusing more on your fear of delivering the speech than on the process of assembling your presentation in the first place.

It is often easy to spot those presentations that have been thrown together at the eleventh hour: they tend to be poorly thought through and badly structured. In my experience the best means of reducing nerves is to gain a sense of control over your presentation and the material it contains; and in this instance that control is best obtained by knuckling down to deal with the task at hand.

It may be easier said than done, but instead of wasting time worrying, you should immediately start work on your presentation. Aside from avoiding a last minute panic, this will force you to think about what you are going to say, rather than the fear of actually having to say it. Allowing plenty of preparation time will also make you familiar with your presentation and its contents which will in turn make for a more confident delivery.

All presentations, regardless of their complexity, are built around simple objectives. For example, some presentations will want to sell a particular product, message or idea while others may want to inform or educate an audience. Some are there simply to offer entertainment.

Before you start to assemble your presentation, you should sit down and see if you can summarise your entire talk in a single sentence. This may seem like an odd thing to do but condensing your message into a few words should provide you with a central message around which you can build the rest of your speech.

The next job is to look at your probable audience and what they will be expecting from you. You will need to tailor your presentation to your audience in such a way that they will not become confused or bored. This means considering key characteristics such as people's prior knowledge of your subject area, their skill levels, opinions and any likely behavioural issues (e.g. are people likely to heckle?).

With a basic understanding of your audience and your central message decided, you will be ready to start assembling the building blocks of your presentation.

It is unusual for the structure and content of a presentation to enter your head fully formed and it may be necessary to re-order and refine your talk several times before you are happy. Begin by writing down all the central points and facts that you would like to include in your talk. Choose the ones that best support your core message and think about how you can arrange these to form the backbone of your presentation. Sometimes it helps to write your central points on sticky Post-It notes so that you can swap them about until you get the order right.

Do not be tempted to include too much information as this often results in a rushed presentation that is driven by too many visual aids, such as slides. A simple presentation will ensure that the audience can keep pace and will better absorb any points or facts you might want to deliver.

At this stage it may be as well to highlight any subjects or topics that will require additional work or research so that you can factor this into your preparation schedule. You will also need to give some thought to the manner in which you want to deliver your information. For example, will you be able to show computer-generated slides or will you need to prepare acetate sheets for an overhead projector?

Writing your speech: putting flesh on the bones

Hopefully it will not have taken you too long to put together a basic outline of your presentation; now you must add flesh to its bones.

To engage an audience there must be a logical flow to your presentation. It can help to think of your presentation as being akin to a short story that has a beginning, middle and end.

At the beginning of your speech you should briefly let your audience know what it is you are going to tell them. Then use the middle bit of your speech to tell them this. Finally, at the end you should finish by summarising what it is you have just told them.

In other words, use the first part of your presentation (*the opening*) to outline your subject area, your relationship to it and the reason why you want to talk about it. The central section (*the body*) should be used to deliver the main part of your presentation with its accompanying facts and figures. In the last section (*the summary*) you should bring together and précis everything you have just said, highlighting those points that you want people to remember.

The opening

The opening part of your speech sets the stage for what is to follow. It introduces your audience to the subject of your presentation and the reason you want to speak about it. You should also present a brief summary or outline of the main points that will be covered. This will help to keep your audience oriented within the framework of your script.

It sometimes helps to begin a presentation with an image, fact or statement that is arresting or controversial to grab the audience's attention. Other tried and tested methods of gaining people's attention is to start a presentation with a personal anecdote that explains your interest in your topic. However, make sure the anecdote is interesting, relevant and short: there is nothing worse than beginning a talk with an overlong and boring story.

Starting out with a question can be a good way of engaging your audience. Ask them a relevant question to which they will want to know the answer. You can then use your presentation to gradually answer it, with the ultimate solution coming at the end.

The body

This is the part of the speech in which the bulk of your subject matter will be presented. The body is longest part of your speech and so it should be separated into smaller, easily assimilated modules. Each module or sub-section should make a single point or convey one idea, like a chapter in a book. Sometimes these sub-sections can each have their own simple opening, body and summary but do not make them overlong: with speeches too much detail is often less interesting.

The summary

This portion should be brief and simple. Here is your chance to reinforce the central theme and purpose of your presentation. Briefly emphasise the key points and main ideas of your script in this section.

By structuring your speech into these three parts, the audience should know where you are going and roughly where they are in your overall presentation.

Always consider what are the most effective ways to organise your speech in order to adapt it to the purpose, people, place, etc. This will not only help you structure the presentation, but it will help the audience to understand it.

Bear in mind that while graphs and lists are useful ways to communicate hard facts, most audiences will respond well to a more descriptive speaking style. Short stories and anecdotes are a great way of solidifying something into your audience's mind, and they encourage interaction.

Finally, when you have pulled all your basic information together and have a draft structure for your speech, you can think about the sort of visual aids you could use to illustrate the points you wish to make.

Visual aids: keep it simple

Visual aids should be used principally to assist the audience to interpret or clarify the information you are telling them. This section contains advice on how to avoid turning your presentation into a random assortment of bullet-pointed lists by ensuring that your visual aid will help, not hinder, your presentation.

People will learn and understand information more readily when it is presented to them in a clear and interesting visual manner. However, if you simply use visual aids as means of filling slides with acres of dense text or lists, then you will soon lose your audience.

In the days before computers the inclusion of visual aids in a presentation was a time-consuming process that meant manually creating overhead slides or filling carousels with photographic slides. Many presentations simply relied upon people writing on a blackboard or paper flipchart. The digital age means that colourful, creative slides displaying photos, sound and film clips can be generated in minutes. However, this can be a curse as well as a blessing and many a presentation has been ruined by the overuse of graphical gimmicks, silly fonts and unnecessarily crowded and complex slides.

When it comes to visual aids the general rule is to keep it simple. Do not set out to impress your audience with fancy graphics. The days of people being impressed by flashy computer slides have long since passed so concentrate on using your visual aids to complement your central objectives.

When creating slides, use as few words as possible. Each slide should have fewer than forty words on it; any more than this and your audience will either not bother to read it or, if they do, they will not be listening to you. People are only going to remember the central facts so keep it simple. Remember, you do not need a transcript of your speech on your slides!

Use a minimum point size of 24 or even 30 and use lower case letters. Capitals should only be used for abbreviations. Use a sans serif font for titles and for chart labels (e.g. Arial) and a serif font (e.g. Times New Roman) for bullet points or body text.

A bullet-pointed list of independent clauses should use initial capital letters: a list of words or phrases should not. Avoid paragraphs or long blocks of text and detailed reports. If you need to include a report, hand it out and then refer to it. Do not cram slides with concepts: if you have three points to make then use three separate slides.

When it comes to animations and video, remember that less is more. While movement does attract attention, doing it to excess will actually distract people from your message. A basic dissolve from one slide to another is sufficient. Video is complicated and, unless it is absolutely integral to the presentation, this is best avoided by novices.

Use images where you can as these will help you to connect with your audience. This is particularly true where you have an audience where English is not their first language. Try to include some light-hearted photographs, images or cartoons at key points in your talk as these will revive people's interest in what you are saying. Think carefully about what you put on your last slide as this will often be on screen for some time, especially if you are taking questions from the audience.

With regard to this last point. It is a good idea to try to anticipate any questions that the audience might want to ask you and to prepare for them. If necessary have a cue card that has some additional facts and figures that might be needed to answer a particular question.

Rehearse: practice makes perfect

Rehearsing a presentation is not an easy or particular desirable thing to do but it is a vital part of the speech writing process. Do not fall into the trap of thinking that running through your presentation a couple of times while on your own will do the trick. The rehearsal process should begin as soon as you have put together the basic outline of your presentation.

The purpose of a rehearsal is not just to familiarise yourself with what you are going to say. It is also a mechanism for spotting flaws and errors in your presentation that may not otherwise be obvious. On a basic level it will let you know whether your presentation is too long or too short for the time allotted; whether you have too many or too few visual aids; and whether you are repeating yourself or making aspects of your presentation unnecessarily complicated.

Thus your rehearsals should begin early on. Your first rehearsals should be performed on your own. This allows you to stop to make notes/adjustments or to correct your mistakes as you go along. Use these rehearsals to get the content and visual aids correct; think of them as being part of the script-writing process rather than just a last minute run through.

As you are doing your first rehearsals make notes of the key points of your presentation on blank postcards. These will be used later on as cue cards. Do not be tempted to write too much on your cue cards: you want simple bullet points that can found and read at a glance. Long sentences on a cue card cannot be deciphered at speed and will only confuse and fluster you.

Keep an eye on timing. This is not so relevant in the first couple of rehearsals as you are bound to want to stop and correct something or other. However, when you think you have a finalised script and visual aids, you should do a full run through against the clock. At this stage it can help to have a small audience as this will force you to focus on them, rather than just the content of your presentation. The audience does not need to know anything about your presentation; they are there to help you concentrate.

Pay attention to the timing of your rehearsals. Do not assume that if you are ten minutes over the allotted time, that you can sort this out on the day. In my experience, most rehearsals tend to be 10 to 15 percent faster against the clock than the actual delivery. Therefore if I have to give a presentation of say, 40 minutes duration, I am happy if the rehearsal comes in at around 30 to 35 minutes. It is better to be marginally too short than too long.

An alert person's attention span is around 40 minutes but a good many people in your audience will have an attention span that is shorter than this. If you are talking after lunch or at the tail end of a two or three day symposium then people's attention span will also be shortened.

To avoid sleeping delegates, be clear what you want to include in your presentation (especially during the first twenty minutes) and what cannot be accommodated. Leave plenty of time for discussion during and at the end of the presentation.

In a spare moment, look through your cue cards and visual aids. This will help embed the important parts of your speech in your head. Hopefully all this practice will have familiarised you with your presentation to such a degree that you need not worry too much about what you are going to say. Below are a few more pointers you might want to think about while rehearsing your presentation.

You should try to adjust your tone and delivery to your subject matter so consider what style of delivery is best suited to the purpose of your speech. Is your presentation about a sombre subject (e.g. pollution, war) or something more optimistic, such as a solution to a problem? Practice adopting the correct tone and, if necessary, practice smiling or delivering emphasis at key points.

Use your body as a visual aid. Gestures can help to emphasise or explain key points so be mindful of your hands and do not keep them folded in front of you. If you need to, use one hand for gestures, and keep the other one in your pocket. Feel free to move about the stage but do not pace.

Avoid colloquialisms and clichés such as 'like', 'goes', 'you know', 'at the end of the day', 'err' and 'um'. This is not to please the grammar police but instead to make your presentation sound more professional and less like an after-match interview.

Keep a glass of water handy. If you get stuck for words then take a drink of water to buy some thinking time. You could also take a drink after making an important point to allow time for it to sink in.

Delivery: facing your audience

The big day has arrived. All the hard work of researching, writing and preparing your script and slides is behind you. Now it is time to share it with your audience. This section will cover key presentational techniques to help you and the audience get the most out of the occasion by developing your relationship. It is a performance so remember to pace yourself and to enjoy the experience.

Leave absolutely nothing to chance. Arrive at the venue early so as to give you enough preparation time. Review the space, audio-visual facilities, lighting, audience and any last minute changes to the schedule.

Find out what style of microphone (if any) you will be expected to use. A clip-on microphone can take a couple of minutes set up so make sure that it is in place before you go on stage. Be wary of turning your head when using a clip on microphone as this may move your mouth out of its range.

Even with a microphone you will need to speak clearly and slightly louder than normal. If there is no microphone then project your voice to the back of the auditorium by speaking slowly and loudly with your head up and facing the audience. Remember to remove and/or turn the microphone off when your talk is finished. You do not want to be caught saying something inappropriate off stage.

Check which issues other speakers are due to cover just in case you can link these with your talk. Make a note of the names of key people and other speakers; you may need these later. If necessary be prepared to make last minute minor adjustments to your talk.

Before you walk on to the stage, relax. Unlock your knees and shake out your arms. Breathe from your stomach, rather than your chest. Before you speak, first take a slow deep breath and slowly breathe out again.

People naturally respond to your cues so engage with the audience by looking at them and smiling. However, they will only be interested in what you have to say if they can hear you so speak slowly and project your voice. A good trick is to look at the back couple of rows and try to deliver your talk to them. Display enthusiasm and passion.

Eye contact is important when you are trying to engage an audience. At times look up and make eye contact with various people in the audience. It is a form of visual handshake and shows that you, yourself are engaged with the topic. However, be careful not to make contact with the same person too often and do not stare.

When speaking to small groups it is possible to engage them by asking the audience leading questions and then soliciting answers from them. This 'who can tell me...' approach can work with small groups but it does require a degree of self-confidence. You must also be careful not to sound too much like a teacher addressing a group of schoolchildren.

To keep the audience on your side, make your presentation all about them. Connect every point back to the people sitting before you. Why should they care about what you are saying? How does it benefit them? For every main point you have, you should be able to answer the 'so what?' question.

Refer to specific people, places, statistics and situations as you talk but do not bombard people with information. This is especially true of statistics which can become meaningless if delivered too quickly and too often.

It is better to present a set of results without all the workings behind it: tell the audience that you will provide more details to interested individuals. If you notice that the audience's attention is wandering then try to move on to your next point or, if necessary, shorten the presentation. Conclude the presentation with a summary of the key points before asking for questions. If you or your company has a website then make sure that your last slide clearly displays your www address and/or any other contact details such as an e-mail address.

Question and answer sessions

You should allow time for questions. In most circumstances ten minutes should be ideal but adjust this to suit your venue, audience and allotted time. Make a request for questions and then wait a few seconds for people to raise their hands.

In most instances you will be faced with several people with their hands up and it will be up to you to pick your questioner. When you choose someone make sure they know you have picked them. Point to the person and briefly describe them (in flattering terms): 'The man in the red jumper...', etc. Some larger auditoriums have a microphone for the audience so it may be necessary to wait for this to reach the questioner.

If no hands go up then do not panic. This may reflect an audience's shyness rather than the quality of your presentation. In this situation you can sometimes prompt questions by making a joke of it ('I've clearly stunned you into silence...') or by asking yourself a question ('One point I was going to make...' or 'I am surprised that no one picked up on the following point...'). If this does not work then simply end your presentation.

You should already have made an attempt at anticipating your questions (see earlier) so hopefully there will not be any nasty surprises. If you are confronted with a question to which you do not have an answer then admit this and ask the questioner to leave their contact details so that you will get back to them later. In this circumstance make sure that you do get back to the questioner: in a sales scenario, this is very important.

Do not be frightened to cut a questioner short, especially if they attempt to engage you in a prolonged debate or discussion. Explain that you want to hear a range of questions and that you will speak with them afterwards.

Keep an eye on the time. When you have two or three minutes left, state that you will take one more quick question and, having done so, close the session. Thank the audience for their attention and participation and wish them a good day/evening. This is their cue to show their appreciation, after which you should gather your materials and leave the stage.

Make yourself available after your presentation as people might want to speak with you in private. If you think your presentation will attract a lot of attention then it may be worth having some handouts or brochures prepared or perhaps even putting a copy of your presentation on the Internet (but be careful not to infringe the copyright on any images you have used).

Top Tips

- Begin preparing your presentation straightaway. Do not delay!

- Structure your presentation carefully. Make sure that it is clear, logical and progresses from one point to the next.

- Avoid too many slides, too many bullets, and too much text.

- Wherever possible give personal illustrations. The best funny anecdotes are the ones you tell against yourself, they seldom fail and they get the audience on your side from then on.

- The rule of three makes it easy for people to remember points. Good speeches are peppered with three item lists: Friends, Romans, Countrymen; Blood, sweat and tears.

- Rehearse on your own to begin with in order to refine your presentation. Pay attention to timing.

- Use bullet-pointed cue cards, not a script.

- Speak clearly. Be prepared to adapt what you have to say at the last moment to accommodate your audience.

- Do not be afraid to state what is obvious to you, it may be news to the audience.

- Before you speak, first take a slow deep breath and slowly breathe out again.

- Be optimistic and smile. Make eye contact, especially when you are stressing a key point.

- Have some water ready.

- Prepare answers to obvious questions. If necessary prepare handouts or place a version of your presentation on the Internet.

- In the face of hostile questioning, invite comment from the audience. Steer hostility away from you.

- Remember the 'three Es': Energy; Enthusiasm; Excitement.

The Business Pitch
How to Pitch to an Investor

- Basic Preparation
- The Pitch Book
- During the Pitch
- Afterwards

Fund raising is a necessity for most small and medium-sized businesses and a traditional means of attracting an investor is to organise a business pitch. In its simplest terms, this is a meeting between you and your would-be investor(s) during which you provide a presentation that will convince them to part with their cash. This is, of course, much easier than it sounds, especially in these austere times.

A competent business pitch can be a make-or-break moment for a company and for the careers of the individuals making the presentation. For a small or growing business, a successful pitch can bring in valuable funding, create new orders and help you to gain the attention of potential new clients. Within larger organisations it can be used to steal a march on competitors and to open doors to all kinds of new ventures and opportunities. These are the sorts of prizes that we are aiming for.

Conversely, an incompetent pitch, especially a badly delivered one, can be a frustrating and embarrassing experience which might mean the loss of new business opportunities as well as a sense of personal disappointment at a lot of effort wasted. I speak from personal experience.

Several years ago my employer was invited to address a small gathering of professionals with the aim of attracting more business for my company. I was experienced at pitching for business and, blinded by confidence and the thought that I was addressing only a few people, I failed to do much preparation.

Instead of researching my venue and developing a slick pitch which would suit the occasion, I simply pulled together a few overhead slides against which I planned to deliver an off the cuff talk. Needless to say, I did not put together an executive summary or a pitch book (see below) as I had persuaded myself that it was not appropriate for the occasion.

On the big day I arrived just ahead of my slot only to find a dozen potential clients sitting down in complete silence, listening to the closing words of the previous speaker. He was addressing them from a podium at the front of a small auditorium and as I waited, I became nervous and started to regret my arrogance.

I was introduced and walked to the podium, frantically turning over in my mind what I was going to say and how I would begin my talk. What followed was a fumbled, disjointed presentation that neither looked nor sounded professional. After five minutes one attendee interrupted to ask me a question that I had no answer for. Then the projector stopped working.

Trust me when I say it went downhill from there. It was an experience that neither I, nor my employer, would wish to be repeated. I was determined it would not happen again and ever since I have always prepared diligently ahead of any public speaking engagement.

Basic preparation

The key to any successful pitch is preparation. And lots of it. This should begin immediately. Once you know you are going to have to make a pitch, start preparing. Do not put it off for weeks or even days, especially if you are planning to produce a pitch book (see below) for your potential clients. However, before you put pen to paper there are some fundamental things you will need to think about.

Know your venue
Will your pitch be made in a small and intimate meeting room or a large (and probably impersonal) auditorium?

This will depend on the scale of your pitch. If you are addressing a national or international conference with a large audience, then your pitch will most likely take the form of a business presentation. If so then you should also bear in mind some of the advice about business presentations given in Chapter 3 of this book. In this chapter we shall be focusing on smaller, more intimate pitches made to a selected audience of perhaps ten to thirty people.

If you are speaking to a small audience then try to get a suitably-sized venue arranged, such as a meeting room rather than a lecture theatre. However, the choice of venue may be out of your control so be prepared for all eventualities but do make sure that the venue is at least big enough for your needs. If you think you will need a bigger venue then say so to the organiser as having people standing at the back while you are speaking may be off-putting.

Most importantly, check that the venue has all the facilities that you will need especially if you are using computer-generated visual aids. Check their IT set up and ask which software packages they have available. Ask what format you will need and whether computer files must be brought on a CD-ROM, memory stick, etc. Check whether there will be a technician present. If not, then consider bringing a laptop with you - if you are in a small venue and all else fails you can deliver the presentation on this.

Are you pitching alone or with others?

Some pitches are made by individuals but within a business setting it is not unusual for a presentation to involve two or more people. The largest group I have worked with is nine; the smallest is three. Working in a small team can help ease the nerves and spread the workload but it brings with it other issues you should be aware of.

If working in a small team then you should all meet at the earliest opportunity, perhaps in an informal setting, in order to work out what your objective is and who is going to do what to achieve this.

The theme and outline of the pitch should be decided as a team. You should then divide up the work among yourselves and create an agreed timetable for delivery. Place one person in charge of overseeing the team's activities and arrange to have regular progress meetings (individually and as a team). If you are not the one in charge of organising, then make sure you understand how you and others are expected to contribute to the pitch, and in what order.

It sometimes helps to take someone senior with you, especially if you have the CEO of a company in the audience. There are times when a bit of grey hair can make a good impression.

Understand your audience

Will the people you are pitching to be senior or junior, experienced or inexperienced in your field, etc.? Do you know any of them? Are all of them fluent in the language that you will be speaking in?

Have you or any of your team previously worked with the individuals you are pitching to? If so then draw on this knowledge and use it as a way of establishing your credentials early in the pitch.

Are you pitching against competitors?

It would be unusual if you were not competing with someone else so if you are pitching for a specific piece of business then it is possible that your audience will already have seen several pitches.

Use what time you have been allocated wisely by staying focused on YOUR story. Do not waste time explaining generic material the client already knows. DO NOT go out of your way to be negative about other companies or individuals that you know or suspect are also pitching. This is a weak tactic that often backfires. Focus on your positives and avoid negativity.

How much time do you have to make your case?

This is crucial. Do not try and cram a 90 minute presentation into a one hour time slot. This tactic never works. Instead, plan your time carefully.

I have seen pitches lost because the presentation ran for an hour leaving the clients bored and with no time for questions. If you have a one hour slot then do not talk for more than 40 to 45 minutes. Go over 50 minutes and you are really in trouble.

A one hour time slot could be imagined as follows:

- to 5 minutes for introductions (and distribution of business cards).
- 35 to 40 minutes on the presentation and the pitch.
- 10 to 15 minutes for questions

What time of day is it?

This might sound facetious but it matters. Pitching very early or late in the day can be difficult, especially in the afternoon when the audience may be tired and easily bored.

You might also struggle with a time slot immediately after a refreshment break or lunch, as digesting food (or any alcohol imbibed) can make an audience sleepy, or on a hot and sunny day when people will want to be outdoors.

If at all possible then try to get a time slot in the mid morning or mid afternoon. If this is not possible then keep an eye on your audience; if it looks as though they are flagging, and it seems appropriate, then stop speaking and ask if anyone has any questions. This brief change in pace will cause people to sit up and pay attention to you and so should revive their attention for a few minutes longer.

Clear the diary
Make sure you have ample spare time on the day of the pitch. Do not schedule your biggest pitch of the year thirty minutes after you land at the airport. Clear out conflicts from the diary and focus on the job in hand.

Where relevant, tell colleagues you are busy and cannot be contacted. Build in spare time to allow for delays and make sure everyone in your team is aware of timings, venue location and what they are supposed to be wearing. Make sure you have each other's mobile and other contact details, in case of emergency.

I will say this again later - but turn off ALL mobile devices and gadgets before you walk in. Do not even leave them on vibrate.

The pitch book

In most small to medium-sized business pitches I have attended, the presentation has been accompanied by a pitch book.

A pitch book is a bound document of between thirty and seventy pages that contains some or all of the main points covered in your presentation. These will be handed out to delegates both to impress them but also so that they can remember what it was you were speaking about. Pitch books are often visual affairs which contain a minimum of text but have lots of colour graphs, tables and photographs.

Creating a pitch book

As well as being a good marketing tool, a pitch book is also a useful means of preparing for your presentation. If you are pitching as a team then one of the first priorities is to decide collectively what should be in the pitch book (and therefore also your presentation) and how it should be presented.

As a team you should create a logical structure for your pitch book/ presentation, then decide who is going to prepare which parts of the pitch. Decide deadlines and assign these to individual team members.

Nominate one person to be in charge of bringing the text and figures together into one document. This person does not need to be a professional designer: their role is to gather all the contributions together on time and to be in charge of quality control. Once the text and figures are all in, it may be necessary to employ a professional designer/publisher to produce the final pitch book. Do not make your pages crowded and avoid long sections of text; bullet points will often suffice. Less is more and giving too much information will confuse people.

Do not prepare your pitch at the last minute. Prepare well ahead and, when you have produced a pitch book, make sure that you and your team learn it by heart so that you know the page order and what is coming next.

If your pitch book does not extend to thirty pages then do not panic. In most pitch books it is only the opening few pages that will contain a key message. The remainder is frequently made up of appendices displaying graphs, tables and various facts and figures.

Make sure that each team member has a copy of the pitch book. Make notes in the margin as to what you want to say or refer to on each page. Make sure that your colleagues do this also and that they know the bits to which they will be contributing.

Practice and content

In the week before the pitch, get your team into a room and practice your presentation. Do this more than once. Practice is important; it not only creates a more polished performance, but will highlight any deficiencies in your content and presentation technique and allow you to amend them. When practicing think about your Unique Selling Point. Make sure you have something concrete to say about WHY your proposition should be the preferred option. Try and structure your pitch so that if one of the audience has to leave early or is dozing off, they can still remember the thrust of your argument.

Understand your personal experience and knowledge levels. If you comprehend the underlying concepts well, then focus your effort on optimising the delivery and style of your pitch. If the subject is not as familiar, then devote extra time to understanding it. Nothing will lose you a pitch faster than demonstrating that you do not know your subject matter.

Visual aids

Visual aids are undoubtedly useful but they can all too easily become problematic due to equipment incompatibility or computer glitches. If you are going to use visual aids then be prepared for that outcome!

A pitch book will often contain many of your slides and so, in the event of equipment failure, you can still talk by referring to specific pages in the book. If you are not using a pitch book then it can be an idea to bring along print-outs from your slides. Equipment failure is a common problem and it pays to ask ahead of time if there will be an engineer on site to fix any problems that might occur.

Even if a slide show runs perfectly, it could have the effect of sending your audience to sleep. Having more than one person delivering the pitch will help keep an audience's interest; so will periodic breaks to ask the audience if there are any questions. Having a pitch book to hand out to the audience as it gives them something to look at while you are speaking.

Appearance is key

If suits are required then wear your best one. Wear a good shirt and tie combination. Polish your shoes. If suits are not required then wear smart casual clothes (i.e. not jeans and trainers) or put on a suit anyway. If you know that you look smart and professional then this will give you added confidence.

Adjust your clothing to the time of year and try to stay cool. There is nothing worse than arriving at a well heated conference room for a pitch and finding you are wearing a thick suit and sitting in the sun.

Body language

Sit up straight in your chair and look people in the eye. Pay attention to the conversation when others are speaking. Do not slouch, yawn, look bored, fiddle with your pen or make doodles on your pad.

If you are tired from a flight or have a hangover then grit your teeth. Do not drink alcohol and avoid too much water or coffee as it may not be possible to visit the toilet just before your pitch. If you find you are very nervous and your hands are shaking then hold a pen. Avoid excessive jollity but some light-hearted interjections can be fine if you think it appropriate.

During the pitch

At the start of your pitch thank the audience for the opportunity to make your presentation - this is essential. At all times be polite. When appropriate, shake hands, exchange business cards and hand around your pitch book. Ideally the most senior person from your team should do this.

Once seated, introduce yourself and any colleagues that are in the room and briefly describe their role and credentials. When multiple nationalities are involved, tell your audience which language you are going to present in and apologise if this is not ideal for everyone.

Tell the audience how you plan to proceed and, if necessary, refer to, or distribute copies of your pitch book. In some cases the pitch book is barely referred to. In others, the audience will want go through it page by page. Ask the clients which they would prefer. If there are time constraints, then suggest skipping sections in favour of the most relevant pages.

If you can make your pitch interactive then do so. A good means is by asking your audience to feel free to interrupt with questions; in doing so you are engaging them in your pitch.

Style, delivery and communication
Arrive early, at least twenty minutes. DO NOT arrive late. Aside from being rude and giving a bad impression, it will make you flustered and on the back-foot.

Try not to read from a script as it will make your pitch sound unrehearsed and monotonous. Sufficient practice should negate the need for a script but if you do not feel confident then the use of cue cards is perfectly acceptable. For further details on cue cards and other prompts see Chapter 3.

Speak more slowly than you normally would. Talking slowly gives your audience time to digest what you are saying and to make notes. You will have to make a conscious effort to do this as people have a natural tendency to speed up during presentations, especially if they know their material well. Talking quickly is also a sign of stress and may make your pitch feel rushed: your audience could pick up on this.

It is IMPERATIVE you turn off all mobile devices before walking into the room. A mobile phone ringing or vibrating during a key part of your pitch will ruin a lot of hard work.

Questions
As part of your preparation, you and your team should make a list of the more obvious and predictable questions that could be asked. It is worth spending time on this because if you stumble at the first question, your

pitch could lose credibility. If your credentials are strong in some areas and weak in others, then concentrate on your deficiencies.

Try to give honest answers and never attempt to brush off a direct question. Do not promise something that you cannot possibly hope to deliver. If you do not have a fact or figure to hand then offer to provide the questioner with this information later on or refer them to a section in your pitch book that has the information they want.

Afterwards

Following the pitch you and your team should make sure that you are approachable by others. If you are at an all day event then at lunchtime and during coffee breaks you should not sit or stand in a tight huddle. Instead try and mingle or at least situate yourselves somewhere where others can easily approach you (e.g. in the centre of a room, rather than jammed in a corner). Have a ready supply of business cards and/or promotional material available to hand out.

You should maintain a professional appearance until you are out of sight and earshot of all other delegates. After delivering a successful pitch there is always a sense of release and relief and so your team might be in the mood to celebrate. If there is an evening function or a social event associated with your pitch then be careful. Make sure that you and your team stay in control of your faculties, especially if alcohol is involved. The lively antics of an employee who has spent too long near the hotel bar can ruin several weeks of hard work.

Handling the Media
Make Sure that Publicity Works for You

- An Unexpected Interview with a Journalist
- A Planned Interview on Radio or Television
- Creating a Press Release
- Nurturing Media Relationships

Is all publicity good publicity? This question reiterates one of the most famous business sayings but if you were to ask this of the directors and shareholders of BP during the spring and summer of 2010, then the answer would be a resounding 'NO!'. And for good reason.

On 20th April 2010 BP's *Deepwater Horizon* oil rig exploded killing several workers and subsequently spilling 50,000 barrels of oil a day into the seas of the Gulf of Mexico. It was one of the worst environmental disasters of modern times which was seemingly exacerbated by BP's apparent inability to stem the flow of oil.

The situation dragged on for months attracting hostility towards BP from every quarter. The *Deepwater Horizon* fiasco quickly turned one of the world's largest oil companies into an American nightmare. BP's shares went into freefall and the company's reputation worldwide was severely damaged.

Worst still, BP's executives reacted slowly to the situation and, when they did respond, they made a series of public blunders which allowed the media to portray BP as a money grabbing conglomerate that put profits ahead of people's lives. Even after the leaking oil well was capped, BP's reputation continued to be tarnished, especially in the USA where the company's name had become a byword for uncaring capitalism.

It need not have been that way. If BP had reacted more quickly to the crisis, apologised and showed more sympathy towards the situation, then the company might have bought itself some time in which to explain the complexities of the situation.

As it was, BP's reaction was haphazard, disjointed and dispassionate, allowing the media to turn what was already an ugly situation into a full blown witch-hunt. The American President bought into the media hostility, demanding that 'heads roll' and that the oil company pay billions in compensation. The head that did eventually roll was that of the BP boss Tony Hayward; he was a victim of his own poor reaction to the explosion and oil spill in what had been a total PR disaster.

But not all disasters need to end in such heartache. Compare BP's media reaction to that of a British airline which suffered a fatal plane crash, and you will see that the right response to a sudden disaster can help to limit any subsequent PR damage.

In January 1989 a British Midland Boeing 737 had just taken off from Heathrow bound for Ireland when it developed an engine fault. It was diverted to East Midlands Airport but as it neared the runway the second engine failed causing the plan to crash onto the M1 Motorway, near Kegworth. Forty-seven of the 126 passengers died and a further seventy-four were severely injured. It transpired that, following the failure of one of the plane's two engines, the pilots had mistakenly shut down the one remaining working engine, causing the plane to crash. It was a case of pilot error, a situation that had the potential to dent British Midland's reputation.

Emergency response personnel were not the only people that rushed to the scene. The media descended in droves, but then so did representatives from the airline, including Sir Michael Bishop, British Midland's chairman. Only a short time after the disaster Sir Michael was being interviewed live on television and in slow measured terms his was the voice of reason and reassurance.

Sir Michael was quick to acknowledge the scale of the tragedy, and to express his sympathy to the relatives of those who had died. He stressed that all would be done to establish the cause of the crash and outlined measures that his company was already taking to make sure that everyone was being kept abreast of developments. Live on television he gave out details of a special hot-line set-up for relatives of passengers and in the following days Sir Michael was always available for interview during which he did not shirk his responsibilities or seek to divert blame onto others.

Sir Michael's actions forced the media to report factual information provided by his company and in doing so reigned in the reporters' natural instinct to indulge in speculation and fault finding. By allowing the media to report the crash accurately, Sir Michael provided some space for the families of those caught up in the tragedy. It was afterwards acknowledged that Sir Michael's prompt reaction to the Kegworth air disaster was a textbook example of how to deal with the media and all the pressures normally associated with that sort of exposure.

But what Sir Michael did was not rocket science. He was merely putting into practice a considered media strategy that provided the journalists with the information and soundbites that they needed while also imparting a clear insight into how the airline was coping with an unexpected tragedy. As business people we all need to be aware of the importance of the media and the importance of developing a good working relationship with them.

The ability to manage the media is not only advantageous to journalists but also to ourselves as it can ensure our market and our stakeholders have an informed view of just what we are doing. And remember, it is a free resource that can positively promote our business activities to a much wider audience.

When thinking about any media campaign or interview, it is important to remember at the outset that newspapers, television and radio stations all have airtime and column inches to fill. And, in these days of ever reducing budgets, many media outlets are also woefully understaffed which means they appreciate all the help they can get, whether that is in the form of a well crafted press release or an interview.

An unexpected interview with a journalist

It is worth spending some time considering your position with regard to media relations. If a journalist phones asking awkward questions about your business, will you be ready? Remember that there could be a great deal riding on your response. So, what should you do when that phone call comes?

Your first priority is to buy yourself some time. An unexpected phone call or visit from a journalist can be an unnerving experience and, rather than answering questions straight away, it is a good idea to have a few moments to collect your thoughts.

Most first contacts with journalists will come via a phone call (although e-mail is becoming more common, so beware about leaving personal contact details on websites). In this situation stall the journalist by asking for the name of their publication, the name of their editor and their contact details, including a phone number. Then ask them about the general nature of their enquiry.

Once you have this information, tell them that you will need to verify this and that you will call him/her back after a set period of time (e.g. ten minutes, half an hour, etc.; but do not make it too long).

Your first priority should be to confirm that the journalist is legitimate. The easiest means of doing this is to search for their name on the Internet. If it is a common name, such as John Smith, then you may need to add into the search engine their name plus the name of their newspaper and/or other keywords such as 'journalist'. So many people put so much information about themselves on Facebook and other social networking sites that it is remarkable what a simple Internet search can turn up.

Having background information about the journalist can be very useful. For example, I was once in a situation where I was contacted by a journalist claiming to work at a national newspaper. An Internet search revealed that he was a trainee journalist on a temporary placement at the paper and that he had put his entire CV on various social networking websites. Knowing that he was inexperienced gave me the upper hand and ensured that the subsequent interview went along the lines that I wanted.

If you find nothing on the Internet then phone the switchboard of the newspaper that they claim to work for and ask if they work there. Sometimes freelance journalists will claim to be working for a newspaper when in fact they are merely fishing for a story. If you cannot find any evidence that the journalist is who they say they are, then ring them back and ask for more details. If they are freelance then find out if they have been commissioned to write the article and how they obtained your contact details. It is vital that you know to whom you are speaking and why they are interested in you. It might be perfectly harmless but it is best to be sure.

While you are doing this, spend a few minutes thinking about the questions that you may be asked and the sort of information you may be asked to provide. If you know why the journalist wants to speak with you then write out some basic notes and have the necessary facts and figures within reach (e.g. a company report). Do not write out pages of notes as you will need to be able to find the information at a moment's notice. Condense your notes onto one page of A4 (preferably on just one side).

Only then should you call the journalist back. When you speak with them, bear the following in mind:

- Do not speak too fast. Speak clearly and simply.

- Do not get sidetracked. Answer any questions directly and succinctly. If it requires a 'yes' or 'no' then say so. Rambling answers will only get you into trouble.

- If you have a message to get across then do not be afraid to repeat it several times.

- Be prepared to answer difficult questions. Do not panic if you do not have an answer to every question; if necessary tell the journalist that you will call them back with the information they want. If you do not feel comfortable answering a question then say so. You are under no obligation to answer every question. Feel free to refer a journalist to other sources of information (such as annual reports, etc.) or to tell them that the information they want is confidential.

- Make sure your answers are in easily understood language. Avoid jargon, abbreviations and technical terms that ordinary members of the public might struggle to understand.

- Always be polite and positive.

- Never go off the record unless you really trust the person to whom you are speaking. You might wish to offer guidance, but make sure that this is understood and not for publication.

- Always try to answer questions. 'No comment' is always an option but it can be portrayed as an admission of weakness or even as an expression of guilt.

- Never be flippant. A throwaway remark can be taken out of context and spoil all the good work that had gone on previously. At the time of the *Deepwater Horizon* explosion Tony Hayward's throwaway remark that he 'wanted his life back' turned a bad situation into an unmitigated disaster.

A planned interview on radio or television

Fortunately an unexpected phone call from a journalist is a rare occurrence. It is more likely that you will be asked to appear as an interviewee on a radio or television programme.

Appearances on broadcast media are usually a routine part of filling airtime and can be a good means of gaining free publicity. However, occasionally you may be asked on air to defend yourself/your company in relation to an incident or accusation. In either instance you should prepare for your interview thoroughly.

Many of the points made earlier about phone interviews apply to radio and television so make sure you do your homework and find out who will interviewing you and what they want to talk about. But there are other issues to bear in mind such as:

- Check whether your interview will be pre-recorded or live. During pre-recorded interviews, especially on radio, if you mess up an answer then you can sometimes ask the interviewer if you can do it again. Check whether this is possible before the interview commences. In my experience television companies are much more reluctant to do this as it is more difficult to edit with pictures and sound. Obviously this is not an option during a live interview.

- Ask the interviewer what their first question will be or if there is anything specific they want you to talk about. That will give you a little time to be ready with an answer and help you deal with any early nervousness. Some interviewers will not provide questions in advance as it is sometimes viewed as poor journalistic practice.

- Check whether anybody else (e.g. a rival or opponent) will be interviewed on the same subject as you. Also ask about the context in which your interview will be used. For example, will it be used as part of a wider feature or will it go out on its own.

- Ensure all any statements put to you during an interview are correct. If a fact or statement is not true then refute it. If you are unsure, then tell the interviewer that you will have to check on it. This may cause the interviewer to ask you to comment on a statement or fact 'on the assumption that it is true'; it is better not to do this but sometimes not providing any answer at all can make it appear that you are avoiding addressing an inconvenient truth.

- If you are being interviewed on the radio then it is usually perfectly acceptable to have a sheet of notes with you. I usually ask if a radio interview can be conducted by phone partly because it avoids the hassle of travelling to a studio but also because it allows me to have two or three sheets of notes laid out on the table in front of me.

- If you fluff your lines then correct yourself succinctly and move on. This is a regular occurrence and it rarely sounds as bad as you think. If the programme is being pre-recorded ask if you can repeat the question at the end (see above).

- Try to speak clearly and at your own pace - do not rush an answer. If you do not understand a question then ask for it to be repeated.

- See if you can find clips or podcasts of interviews by the person who will questioning you - make a note of their style and technique and prepare accordingly.

- You will occasionally find yourself confronted with aggressive interviewers, even on local radio and television. They will typically ask you loaded or outwardly negative questions (sometimes repeatedly) and then cut your answers short, especially if you are not giving them sort of sensationalist material they want. Do not get riled by these tactics. Stay calm and do not be frightened to use those immortal words 'if you would just let me finish...'

- If you get asked the same question repeatedly then do not be tempted to elaborate on a previous answer. Tell the interviewer that you have addressed the point already. If you end up saying this several times in a row then the audience will become more annoyed with the interviewer than you.

- Decide on your core message and make every attempt to get this over to the audience. Then you will have gone a long way towards achieving a real positive for yourself and for those working with you.

It is not easy being interviewed, be it be for newspapers, radio or television and there is often little time to prepare. However, the fact that you have been asked is reason enough to believe that your answers will be important. Even so, it is still worthwhile checking why you have been asked and what the programme might be expecting of you.

Once that has been established it will be up to you to make your answers interesting and easily understood. A good way to do this is by using anecdotes and examples to keep people's attention and, of course, to keep well clear of the sort of business jargon, acronyms and raw statistics that will baffle and irritate an audience.

During the course of any interview do not fidget. Whether on radio or television, keep your hand movements to a minimum so as not to distract the interviewer or the audience. (In the case of radio, fidgeting with pens or paper can sometimes be heard through the microphone.) On television, sit in a relaxed, upright position with your hands in your lap.

Stay focussed on the interviewer as this will keep you focused as well. In the case of television look at the interviewer when speaking, not the camera. The media is a powerful tool for communication but overall success often depends on your attitude.

Creating a press release

It is all too easy to trot out key messages without actually explaining what the messages mean. These sorts of platitudes can annoy both the journalist and the audience and what you have said is likely to have been forgotten once the paper is put down or the set switched off.

That is why it remains important to grab interest straight away. A tested method of doing so is through a press release (also called a news release). Too often you will hear the cry 'we need to market this' when in actual fact what is needed is a humble press release.

A correctly written press release is a cost effective means of conveying important news about products, company personnel or company policy. It is also a way of engaging with local communities and ensuring that people are aware of the work you do.

A press release will typically cover one or two sides of an A4 or A5 sheet of paper. It will probably have a bold headline, one or two introductory paragraphs and then a series of bullet points highlighting key facts or issues.

There is usually at least one image on a press release and the general rule is that they should be simple (i.e. uncluttered) and eye-catching. A journalist will not want to spend twenty minutes reading two pages of dense text in a small unfamiliar font. They will only skim-read most press releases and so must be able to understand your message in only a matter of seconds.

Until recently it was usual for a press release to be drawn up by a specialist public relations firm and then distributed by post or fax. Nowadays budget cuts and advances in computer technology mean that a press release can be created in-house using a word processor or desktop publishing software and then distributed by e-mail or fax. This can save a company a lot of time and money but it necessitates care and forethought as your press release may be competing with a dozen others sat inside an editor's in-box.

Important things to remember when writing a press release are:
- Make your important points at the start and make them eye-catching. If the first couple of lines fail to excite the news desk then your press release will end up in the bin.

- Ensure the communication makes clear it is a Press or News Release. Where possible use a catchy or dramatic headline.

- Ensure the release includes a company logo to help spread brand awareness.

- Try to tell a story, just as you would if you were telling the tale to a friend. The best way of doing all this is to remember who, what, where, why and when. If all can be included then the release will have done the job.

- Use plain language. Avoid jargon and management speak.

- Keep your release brief and to the point.

- Try and include a useable quote from someone within the company. This is particularly important for newspapers as they like to carry at least one quote in an article.

- Try and include a photograph of a product or the spokesperson if necessary.

- Always include a contact name, phone number and e-mail for any follow-up questions.

- Get more than one member of staff to check the press release before it goes live. Mistakes are hard to spot and impossible to correct once the release has been sent out.

When you have your press release ready, draw up a list of media outlets that might be interested in using it. If in doubt then look in a local trade directory or obtain a copy of the latest *Writers' and Artists' Yearbook* as this carries information and contact details for all major and most local media organisations in the British Isles and USA.

Be selective when drawing up your distribution list. Do not send releases out for the sake of it - this is a waste of your time. Target your release carefully and pay attention to local media organisations as they are more likely to respond than the national media. And do not forget the trade papers and journals, most of whom are always after good features and stories.

Sometimes, of course, it is not always good news and there may come a time when you will need to face up to criticism and crisis, but properly approached, such things need not be taxing. If a wrong needs righting, such as a defective product recall, then honesty is the best policy. A quickly issued press release will do much to deflect that criticism and provide a starting point to rebuild any confidence that might have been lost.

In recent years there have been products recalled because they have potentially lethal defects, such as faulty car brakes or appliances that spontaneously catch fire. Most of these recalls were issued via spontaneous press releases which meant that the companies concerned faced up to their responsibilities and took the criticism and financial cost on the chin. However, in a few cases companies tried to hide or disguise their defective products until exposed by the media. In such instances the company invariably faced adverse publicity and their brand suffered as a consequence.

Nurturing media relationships

The public have become wise to (and fed up with) the 'spin culture' that has pervaded government and corporate strategic thinking in recent years. People are particularly suspicious of 'on message' politicians and company spokespeople riding rough shod over public opinion and failing to address real issues and answer questions about them.

To avoid giving the impression of 'spin', it makes sense for companies to nurture relationships within local, regional and national media in order to raise awareness about their services and the work they do. It is important to recognise that effective communication is vital in the delivery of an effective public message. In these days of rolling 24-hour news programmes, the media can be a wonderful ally if it is correctly used and I would recommend that attention is paid as to how best to use the facilities available to us.

A good start is by getting to know your local newspapers and radio stations and, again, to remember that their resources are over-stretched. Often a well-prepared press release and a willingly given interview will be gratefully received. These local news organisations are always looking for 'experts' to quote when needed and a busy news desk will always appreciate a contact willing and able to comment and at a moment's notice.

It is also worth noting that the past decade has seen an upsurge in local radio stations and, while most are music driven, they all have news slots and other opportunities (such as morning news programmes) for longer audio features. Many of these are commercial stations which have a strong following within particular parts of the local community. It therefore stands to reason that an interview with some local radio stations will enable you to reach an audience of a particular age, occupation-type or other demographic.

Most news organisations have active web pages and are on the constant look out for news/feature items. There are very few evening newspapers these days because most have switched to morning publications and so they use their web sites to update their daily news items. These can be additional and valued sources of publicity.

We must remember that to build mutual trust, understanding and a working rapport with the media demands discretion, imagination, honesty and discipline. If we succeed in developing these then we will be well on the way to forging a true bond that can only be good for us, for the media and for the good of our industry.

Part Two
Wedding Speeches

The Father of the Bride
How to Start the Wedding Speeches in Style

- Preparing for your speech
- What to include in the speech

When it comes to weddings, the family of the bride are traditionally given two rather unenviable tasks.

The first is to foot the bill for the wedding (although these days they rarely shoulder the entire bill); the second is that the bride's father (or mother) is the first person to give an after dinner speech.

In recent years there has been so much kudos and anticipation placed upon the best man's speech, that the father of the bride has become rather overshadowed. In some respects this is a blessing, as there is no pressure on the father to be funny or provocative (that is the job of the best man), nor overly flattering (the prerogative of the groom). Instead they are there to speak about themselves and their relationship with the daughter.

To some the father of the bride's speech might appear to be a comparatively easy job but getting the tone, content and length right is not as easy it may first appear. However, there are a few simple rules which, if followed, should enable you to produce a speech which will leave the wedding guests smiling and also set the tone for the rest of the speeches.

Preparing for your speech

Most of us have witnessed the toe-curling consequences of a speaker that has failed to prepare adequately. Public speaking does not come naturally to most people and it is easy to let nerves get the better of you at which time mistakes are easily made. In the context of the father of the bride speech the most commonly made mistakes include:

- Forgetting the name of the groom
- Losing a page of the speech text
- Forgetting key elements/duties (e.g. toasting the bride and groom)

Of course an audience will be indulgent and will forgive a nervous parent's faltering; but with a little preparation your nerves can be minimised allowing you to deliver a polished speech. As with most things in life, the trick is preparation. Hence I advise doing the following:

- Prepare well in advance. Start thinking about your speech at least a month or so before the wedding and have a full draft ready at least two weeks ahead. There will be much to do in the run up to the wedding so do not be tempted to leave it until the last minute.

- Decide whether you are going to speak from prompt/cue cards or to read your speech from a script. This is a matter of personal preference but bear in mind that cue cards will allow you to interact more easily with the guests.

- Feel free to research ideas from different sources but remember that most of your material should be based upon your knowledge and feelings about your daughter. The speech is supposed to be about the bride and her relationship with you and your family.

- Write the speech out in full and practice loud in front of your partner or a close friend. This will enable you to spot any pitfalls (such as awkward words) and to refine the speech. Try to keep the length under ten minutes - people will become restless after this.

- Where possible, co-ordinate the speech with the groom, best man and anyone else who will be speaking. You do not want to overlap too much. Inexperienced speakers will find it hard to adapt at the last minute and may panic if something they were going to say is pre-empted by another speaker. Additionally, all those speaking should agree in advance who is proposing which toasts so that no one is left out.

- If using cue cards then put as few words as possible on them as they are only to be used as a prompt. Number the cards in a top corner (in case they get muddled) and practice using them. If you find you have difficulty with cue cards then consider reading out the speech from a script.

- On the day you will be introduced by the toastmaster (who may also be the best man). Speak slowly and clearly. Look up at your audience periodically as this helps them to empathise with you; it will also help to project your voice.

- Make an assessment of how the room is arranged. It may be that the best place from which to speak is not where you have been seated to eat and drink. Move to a better spot if you think it will help people to see and hear you better.

- Do not drink too much alcohol before speaking - it may remove some nerves but it will make you unsteady, forgetful and careless. It will also mean making more trips to the toilet.

What to include in the speech

There is a traditional structure to the father of the bride's speech which can be followed by those who are new to the process of public speaking. The structure has three parts, each of which will be expanded upon below:

- Introduction: thank everyone for coming.

- Development: talk about the bride and groom, modern marriage and the future.

- Conclusion: propose a toast to the bride and groom.

Introduction

A key thing to remember is that when you stand up, the audience will be on your side and willing you to do well.

The toastmaster should introduce you but if one is not present then, at an agreed point in the proceedings, you should rise to your feet and ask for silence. The floor is then yours.

Before starting your prepared speech, you could make a few off the cuff remarks. For example, you could make some impromptu remarks about events from earlier in the day, such as the venue, or the beauty of the church, or the ladies' stunning hats, or even the state of the weather. Do not appear to be claiming any credit for yourself for things like the quality of the venue or the organisation. Following this your speech could be structured along the following lines.

Thank everyone for coming

This part of the father's speech gets you off to a gentle start. Thank the groom's parents and then all the guests. Make a special point of thanking those who have come the longest distance: this will need some advance research. If applicable, praise the organisation and the chief organiser.

You should then say something complimentary about your daughter and her partner. You could, for example, say how proud you are of them. Then congratulate the groom and say how delighted you are that he will be joining the family and that you look forward to getting to know him and his family. After this you should move onto the subject of your daughter.

Development

This is the part of the speech where you can engage in a little gentle humour but remember that you are not the best man.

Humorous anecdotes are fine but avoid repeating embarrassing stories and risqué jokes: your daughter will not thank you for this. Avoid Internet-sourced jokes and quotes unless you are absolutely sure that you can carry them off. Delivering a joke to an audience is an acquired skill and there is nothing worse than the silence following a failed pun.

Instead of dredging the Internet for material, you could use some of the following themes:

- Mention some of the events that lead up to the wedding, especially if they relate to your daughter. You could describe how and when you first the met groom.

- Tell one or two anecdotes from your daughter's past that illustrate aspects of her development from child to adulthood and her personality. These could be humorous but not embarrassing - if in doubt then check with your partner or a close friend of the family. If possible use these anecdotes to express your feelings towards her.

- Look to the couple's future together. You could say how, even in the modern world, marriage remains an important institution. Offer (helpful) advice about how a marriage can develop and how to make it work (but do not dwell on the hard times). If you want to use quotes or poetry in your speech then this may be the best place to do so.

- Finally, remember that the speech is about your daughter not you. Do not be tempted to use this as an excuse to settle scores against family members (such as an ex-wife) or to waffle on about your own achievements. Keep it to the point and short.

Propose a toast to the bride and groom

Your speech should finish with a toast to the bride and groom. The standard format that everyone will expect is:

'So, ladies and gentlemen, please stand with me as I propose a toast, to the bride and groom...'

The formulation 'please be upstanding' is a little old fashioned but it may suit you and the speech you have given. Once the guests have responded, you can sit down and enjoy the rest of the wedding.

The Groom
Welcome to Married Life

The groom's speech comes in between that of the father of the bride and the best man and it serves two main functions. The first is to thank everyone how has played a part in organising the wedding: this should be done on behalf of both the groom and the bride. The second function is to give the groom an opportunity to introduce the guests to his wife and to tell them how much he loves and appreciates her.

In terms of preparation, the advice offered for the father of the bride's speech in the previous chapter also applies here. To avoid repetition, only a summary of preparation advice is given below, please see the previous chapter for more details:

- Prepare well ahead.

- Decide whether you are going to speak from prompt/cue cards or read out your speech from a script.

- Write out the speech in full and practice it out loud. Try and keep it to between five to ten minutes - people will become restless after this.

- Where possible, co-ordinate the speech with the groom/Best Man/ anyone else speaking. You do not want to overlap.

- Make an assessment of how the room is arranged.

- Do not drink too much wine or beer before speaking.

Introduction

The introduction to your speech should be almost entirely taken up with expressions of gratitude and praise for key participants in the wedding. This could include:

- The father/mother of the bride. Thank him/her for their wonderful speech. You could consider offering a light-hearted reply to some of things they've said. This is best done by picking on one or two comments and offering a quick witty comment. If you are not comfortable with off the cuff remarks or do not think a reply is appropriate, then simply acknowledge the speech and say that you will love and cherish his daughter and endeavour to make her family proud of you.

- Thank the father and/or mother of the bride for consenting to their daughter's marriage.

- Thank the bride's friends and family for welcoming you into their lives and for all their hard work leading up to the wedding.

- Your parents, friends, family and wedding guests. If appropriate then mention your wonderful upbringing by your parents.

- At key opportunities use the expression 'My wife and I...' as this should raise a smile/cheer from the wedding guests. Consider starting the speech with these words but make sure you say it in such a way that people can react by cheering or clapping (e.g. wait until you have everyone's attention, look deliberately at your bride and then turn to the guests and say 'My wife and I...').

Main body

Begin the main part of your speech by talking about your new wife, how lovely she is, and how happy, lucky and proud you are. Address these comments directly to her.

Speak about your time with the your wife thus far. You could illustrate this with a few anecdotes about how you met, your early courting days or things you have discovered about one another.

When choosing stories to tell, use those which are embarrassing or derogatory to you, rather than your new wife. The guests will prefer this and you will remove the risk of upsetting your wife or her family.

Speak about any other people that are important to you and your wife. It could be a sibling or close friend or even someone who is no longer with you. If there are sad things to say (e.g. about someone important who is deceased or could not make it to the wedding) then use these to draw the main part of your speech to a close.

Conclusion

Your speech will finish more or less as it began: with expressions of thanks. In particular the groom should say thank yo to:

- The bridesmaids, ushers and pageboys.
- The best man and ushers for doing their duty so diligently. A humorous remark about the best man's speech could be made at this point (e.g. a plea for leniency).

Hand out any presents to the ushers and bridesmaids (if provided) and offer them a toast. It then only remains for you to thank your guests for attending the wedding. Then turn to your wife and tell her how much you love her and how much you are looking forward to married life. Raise your glass in her honour and sit down.

The Best Man
How Not to Offend Your Audience

- Entertain the whole audience
- Speak to the groom beforehand
- Stay in control

There are any number of ways in which to find content that is entirely unsuitable for a best man's speech. Just go to Google, type in 'best man speech'. Seconds later you will be offered millions of hits, many of which will contain lists of well-worn, often puerile, quotes and jokes that may seem funny on first reading but which will fall flat when the speech is delivered.

So, before you start combing the Internet for that perfect opening line, I would ask that you think carefully about your speech and any offence it might cause. I say this because in recent years there has been a trend towards the best man's speech becoming a laddish affair which seeks to demean or debase the groom through the use of smutty jokes and stories involving drunkenness, sex and poor behaviour.

Speeches like this might appeal to a small (usually male) selection of the audience but they are rarely remembered for being hilarious or entertaining. Indeed, some can be so offensive as to result in members of the audience walking out and/or the end of the best man's friendship with the groom. What should be a happy day can so easily be ruined and all for the sake of a few embarrassed laughs from a minority of the audience.

This chapter asks that you avoid falling into the trap of turning your best man's speech into an x-rated nightmare. Instead of thinking about entertaining your male friends; we ask that you think about everyone who will be in the room and how they will react to your words. Below is some basic advice on how to avoid giving offence during your best man's speech. Please read this before you go off to Google in search of that perfect joke.

Entertain the whole audience

Every wedding has an audience. Most will be a mix of family members plus old and new friends of the bride, groom and their parents. The best man is unlikely to know everybody that's been invited and, unless the gathering is very selective, it should be assumed that you will be speaking to a mix of personalities and ages.

It is a common mistake for the best man to only consider one part of the audience when preparing his speech. In doing so he risks alienating others. If, for example, he aims his speech only at his own peer group, then the result will often be a risqué list of in-jokes and anecdotes that mean little to others and which, in some cases, will cause offence. Equally well, if the best man plays it too safe by tailoring his speech to suit the most easily offended members of the audience, then the result may be bland and disappointing.

Getting the balance right is not easy but a good general rule is to bear in mind that you are trying to please most of the people, most of the time (as opposed to entertaining some of the people, all of the time). Your speech must at some point be able to engage with everybody in the audience which means structuring the speech to be relevant/interesting to as many people as possible.

In this respect you should avoid recollecting embarrassing stories about the groom that do not illustrate a wider point in your speech. For example, telling stories about the groom weeing in a sandpit when he was aged three will say little about his current personality. The same may be true of recalling drunken antics or potentially incriminating incidents which could cause some of the audience to view the groom in a different light. There is a place for embarrassment in the best man's speech but it needs to be done carefully. It is easy to relate stories that will make the groom, his bride and other family members squirm in their seats but often these are not funny. Just as bad is hinting in your speech that the groom had done something terrible in the past but then not revealing what this was. This might cause some sniggers amongst those that know what you are talking about, but it will irritate much of the rest of the audience.

As the next chapter will suggest, it is better to pick a theme for your speech (e.g. the groom is a poor timer-keeper and always late for everything) and to link any anecdotes to this. As best man, your job is to mock the groom in an intelligent, humorous manner: you are not there to humiliate him or to offend the audience.

Equally well, many Best Men begin their speech writing process by making contact with the groom's parents, school friends, work colleagues, etc., to ask for funny tales from childhood, college days or work. While this can be useful in terms of general research (e.g. gaining a wider understanding of the groom's personality), it can be a mistake to build your speech around such anecdotes unless the stories will be understood and appreciated by everyone.

Finally, remember that from the groom's point of view the most important members of the audience are the bride and her parents. This fact should immediately rule out any reference to previous girlfriends, intimate moments between bride and groom or similar comments that could cause embarrassment and/or offence. This is just common sense but it is amazing how many Best men think it is funny to dwell on past relationships.

Speak to the groom beforehand

As best man, it is probable that you will know the groom very well. You do not want your speech to precipitate the end of a beautiful friendship so before putting pen to paper, step back and consider whose day this is: the bride's and groom's.

As best man, your function is to organise the ushers, deliver the ring, as well as to make a speech. In short, you are there to support the happy couple and to help make their day special. This applies as much to your speech as to any other aspect of your duty as best man: therefore do not think about how your speech will reflect on you, think about how it will reflect on the groom, his bride and their close family.

If you are in any doubt then speak to the groom ahead of time. Do not reveal your speech content, but do ask him whether there are sensitive areas to avoid. It is very probable that he will not want you to mention ex-girlfriends but the groom may be aware of other things that will cause offence with the bride or her family (e.g. he may not want to mention how the first met or that they lived together before marriage, etc.).

There may also be aspects of the groom's life that do not seem embarrassing to you but which, for whatever reason, he does not want other people to know about. For example, I was best man at a wedding where the groom asked me not to mention that he was active for a particular political party when at university. It wouldn't have occurred to me that this could have caused him embarrassment so it was good to be forewarned.

That said, most grooms will err on the side of caution and so it is up to you to make a sensible judgement about the material that gets included in your speech. In some cases if you exclude everything the groom does not want mentioned, then your speech will be dull. You must therefore make a judgement based on your knowledge of the groom, the bride and your audience. As outlined above, think about the whole of the audience's reaction to your stories and be especially careful if you are mentioning anything to do with sex, drunkenness or past relationships.

It is probably fair to say that if the groom is a rugby player, with an outgoing and boisterous family, then you will have more license with the material. If you are attending a wedding in which religion or family tensions feature heavily then think carefully before revealing all about the events on the stag night. (Even if the groom is not religious, he or his bride's family might be.)

If in doubt then the safest course of action is to stick to comments that relate to an appropriate trait of the groom that most of the audience can relate to; e.g. is he known for being habitually scruffy/neat/punctual/etc.?

Stay in control

Often the most overlooked part of preparing and delivering a speech is yourself. Few of us are great public speakers and many approach such an occasion with nerves and trepidation. Add to this the fact that the best man's speech will usually take place after a hearty meal at which much wine and other alcoholic drinks might be served, and there is a potential recipe for disaster.

Having a few glasses of wine might calm your nerves but it can also seriously impair your performance and judgement. Drunkenness will make you unsteady, slur your words and impair your concentration and ability to read. It is difficult to disguise being drunk and obviously being so while trying to stumble through your speech will shift the centre of attention away from what you are saying and on to you instead. This will reflect badly on you and your hosts and may be seen as an abuse of their hospitality.

The advice here is simple: steer clear of too much alcohol. One or two glasses of wine spread across a three course meal will do little harm. Drink several glasses and your speech could be remembered for all the wrong reasons. Remember, this is not your big occasion so for the sake of groom and his bride, stay away from the booze and keep control. It is better to be nervy than drunk when speaking.

The best means of avoid nerves is to consider carefully both how you want to deliver your speech as well as what you are going to say. Although you may feel self-conscious doing it, you should practice in advance.

Be it to a friend, relation or just to yourself in the mirror, go through the speech in full several times. This will help embed the material but also help you practice the delivery, when to pause for the jokes, how to deliver some lines quickly and some more slowly.

Most people rely on some form of prompt system, just in case their memory or nerves fail them. Some make notes on a postcards to remind them of key points. Others write a whole script and then read it *verbatim*. A few write a script and then learn it by heart. We are all different but you should use your practice sessions to find out which method suits you.

If nerves are liable to be a real issue then try asking the bride and groom whether they would consider making the speeches before the meal and not after. This breaks with tradition but if you and the other speakers are not natural or confident in the role, you may find that getting the speeches out of the way makes the rest of the day much more enjoyable.

Remember that writing a best man's speech is a bit like the England football team and penalty shoot-outs: there is nothing like the real thing, but practice will make you better!

The Best Man
Writing a Successful Speech

- The Toastmaster
- The Speech: Gratitude and Telegrams
- The Speech: Structure
- Props
- Preparation
- Ending the Speech

Being asked to be the best man at a wedding can be a great honour and yet also a great burden. The honour comes from the groom having deemed that you are the person whom he thinks is best placed to organise key aspects of the wedding. The burden is the best man's speech which in recent times has become a something of a focal point within the wedding celebrations.

The weight of expectation that is placed upon the best man's speech can appear daunting but, as with most forms of public speaking, the task can be made considerably easier by following a few simple rules. This chapter will help guide you through the basics of being a best man and will show you how to assemble the sort of speech that should get a favourable reaction. Follow these rules and the day should run smoothly. You might even enjoy yourself!

The toastmaster

Before you even thinking about writing your best man speech, you need to find out which duties the bride and groom will be expecting you to perform. You will, of course, have a function during the main ceremony (e.g. holding the ring, organising the seating, etc.) but you should also enquire as to what you will be required to do during the wedding meal. Most importantly of all, are the bride and groom expecting you to be the toastmaster?

The toastmaster is the person who stands up, asks for silence and then introduces the speeches. It is possible that someone else might be have been assigned the duty of toastmaster but if not, then the task will probably fall to the best man.

Being toastmaster is not a particularly onerous task and in some respects it benefits the best man by allowing you and guests to become familiar with one another. It also gives you a chance to learn how best to project your voice into the room.

If you are toastmaster then, when the appointed time for the speeches arrives (often after coffee has been served but the groom should indicate this) you will need to stand up and gain the attention of the wedding guests.

Obtaining silence is best done gently. Begin by making your presence felt visually: stand up tall and make sure you have room between you and your chair to take a step backwards. Look across the room at the guests for a few seconds, catching people's eye, then speak loudly and clearly. You may need to say the same phrase (e.g. 'ladies and gentlemen') a few times before there is sufficient hush for you to continue. Once there is hush, raise your glass and say: 'To the bride and groom!'

Take a sip (not a gulp) from your glass and then introduce the first speech. This will normally be the father of bride, followed by the bride groom, and then the best man. However, there may be any number of people speaking including such variations as the mother of the bride, a best woman, etc.

Make sure you know who is speaking and when they are speaking. To introduce each person you should say something along the lines of: 'Ladies and gentlemen; I give you the father of the bride.'

Raise your glass again, then sit down and listen to the speech. When it finishes, stand up, thank the speaker and introduce the next person.

The speech: gratitude and telegrams

Eventually your time to speak will come and at that moment you will be expected to stand up and entertain the guests with a brilliant mixture of insightful wit and pathos before sitting down again to rapturous applause. At least that is what some prospective best men think is expected of them. Thankfully the reality is more mundane.

A best man's speech is more structured than most people realise and, unless you are a confident public speaker, it is wise to build you speech around this structure.

At the start of your speech you will be expected to thank those who have helped organise and pay for the wedding. So, when you stand up to deliver your speech there are certain expressions of gratitude that you will be expected to make on behalf of the happy couple. Check beforehand, but these will normally include:

- Thanking any previous speakers (e.g. the father of the bride).
- Thanking and complimenting the bridesmaids and pageboys.
- Thanking the host and/or hostess. If the host and hostess also happen to be the parents of the bride or groom, then consider offering a toast to them.
- If applicable, then thank the manager of the venue and their staff.

At this point you might also want to raise a toast to the bride and groom, to wish them every future happiness. It is common for presents to be given to certain people, such as the bridesmaids/pageboys; if so then hand these out immediately after you have thanked them.

Once the thank yous are out of the way, you should read out any messages of congratulations, letters and other written contributions that will have been sent in by absent guests.

If there are a lot of these then some editing may be necessary, especially in the case of lengthy letters. Nobody expects (or will want) you to read out a three-page letter so before the ceremony try to find some poignant or funny paragraphs. Mark these with a highlighter pen and read them out.

After you have finished you raise your glass in a toast to absent friends. Then it will be time for your speech.

The speech: structure

Only a handful of people are blessed with the ability to stand up and deliver a brilliant off the cuff speech. The rest of us will need to prepare something in advance and then use cue cards (or similar) to help us remember what to say next.

Possibly the worst part of speech writing is that moment right at the start when you are faced with a blank sheet of paper and no idea what to put on it. Obviously a best man's speech is a personal affair but there are certain themes which may help you to find suitable material. For example, it is common for the best man's speech to include things such as:

- A brief and flattering verbal portrait of the bride which highlights her character, beauty and why she and groom are suited to one another. Perhaps mention her dress (in a complimentary manner) or how you first met her.

- Humorous anecdotes about the wedding preparations. Did anything go wrong? Were you worried that something might go wrong based on your knowledge of the bride or groom (e.g. is the groom always late or forgetful, etc.)?

- A description of your reaction to being made best man. However, keep this brief and/or use it as a means of saying something about the groom. Remember that this speech is not about you!

Mixed in with all this is what is commonly perceived as being the really tricky part of the best man's speech: what to say about the groom.

As ever, common sense is needed here as you do not want to be one of those Best Men who is afterwards ostracised by family and friends because they included offensive or inappropriate material in their speech. The whole of the previous chapter is devoted to the subject of inappropriate material in a best man's speech - read it and make sure that you do not overstep the mark or you will live to regret it.

When it comes to saying something about the groom, it is tempting to reach straight for the Internet in order to search for witty anecdotes and/ or quotations which can be cut and pasted into a speech. There is nothing strictly wrong in doing this, but it is often fairly obvious to an audience when they are being told something that was not written by the speaker or when quotes are used out of context.

My advice would be to try and write something yourself, as the audience will appreciate it more. Your thoughts about the groom will work best if they are structured around a central theme which runs through the centre of your speech and to which you can return periodcially.

Try to find a theme by writing down a list of characteristics that you (and others) most associate with the groom. For example, is he always neatly dressed or is he scruffy? Is he habitually early or late? Is he laid back or highly strung?

Try to choose one or two characteristics that most people will be familiar with and which will give you plenty of scope to say something. These can form the central core of your speech upon which everything else can hang.

The groom's characteristics are an ideal means of introducing humorous anecdotes that can in turn be related back to the wedding procedures. For example, if the groom is always late for meetings, etc., then mention that you were pleased/surprised that he made it to the alter on time - then go on to say that this reminds you of the time you and he nearly missed an important train because the groom had overslept. From this you could then speculate about some aspect of their married life - will the happy couple miss their honeymoon flight? You could emphasise the point by buying an alarm clock and then, at the appropriate point in the speech, awarding it to the groom. Such tactics will give you the mix of embarrassment and humour that the best man's speech requires but without causing offence.

If you are struggling to find suitable characteristics for the groom, then think laterally about the things that you associate with him. For example, think about his hobbies and interests. Is he an obsessive football supporter or fisherman? Does he have an unusual hobby (e.g. I was at a wedding where the groom enjoyed spending nights in haunted houses)? Does he drive a distinctive car? What does he do for a job?

It should be possible to include anecdotes about one or more of these things and to twist them round so that they become relevant to the wedding. Ideally the main part of your speech will only be ten minutes long, and it is surprising how quickly the time will go.

Sometime a prospective best man will ring or e-mail several of the groom's friends and family in search of embarrassing stories. This can be a good means of gauging other people's thoughts about the groom but I would suggest that you only include one or two such anecdotes and that you make sure they are entirely relevant and/or can be used to illustrate a point that your are already making.

Your speech should be an expression of your thoughts and feelings for the groom, not other people's. If you knew the groom as a child then it is entirely appropriate to relate childhood stories as part of a wider theme. If you did not know him as a child then do not spend ages re-telling lots of second-hand childhood stories.

The speech: props

Some Best Men take an alternative approach to their speech by including visual props such as photographs or objects associated with the groom's life.

It is increasingly common to find that the best man has organised a slideshow at the venue or has had photos printed up to a large size. The speech will then be structured around (often humorous) photographs of the groom. Done correctly, this approach can be extremely effective, funny and memorable. When done incorrectly it can be a disaster.

The first thing to remember is that the use of visual aids, such as photographs, is not a substitute for writing your speech. You will still need to have something to say and your speech will still need to be planned around key themes. However, the clever use of pictures can be very effective and will allow you talk about things that would otherwise be difficult, e.g. the groom's dress sense or hairstyles over the years.

Other props can include anything from everyday objects used to illustrate points from your speech (e.g. the alarm clock mentioned earlier) to more elaborate ruses such as a fake awards ceremony.

The golden rules are to use the props sparingly (i.e. do not include too many) and effectively (make sure they conform to a theme and illustrate a point). Finally, as ever, do not include anything that could in any way be conceived as being offensive (pictures of nudity, drunkenness, ex-girlfriends/wives).

The speech: preparation

Writing your speech is only the one aspect of the process; you will still have to deliver it in an audible and effective way. To do so will require you to draw on two essential pieces of advice.

The first of these is rehearsal. This will help tighten your speech and improve your delivery. During the first couple of practice runs you will doubtless become aware of errors or bits of the speech that you are not happy with. Change these as you go along and then keep rehearsing until you have a speech that you can deliver comfortably and confidently. The more you rehearse the more familiar you will be with your speech; if you are worried about sections of your speech then try rehearsing in front of a friend or someone whose opinion you can trust.

A second piece of advice is to avoid reading your speech verbatim from a script. If this is the only way you think you can deliver it then so be it, but a better technique is to get some blank postcards on which you can write the essential points of your speech. With adequate rehearsal these 'cue cards' will act as a prompt to remind you where you are in your speech and what you are supposed to say next. If your speech involves props, such as photographs, then these can often act as a prompt, reminding you what to say next.

The advantage of being able recite some parts of your speech from memory is that it will allow you to look up at the wedding guests periodically. This will help you to project your voice across the room and also to make eye contact with your audience; both will make your speech sound and look better.

The key to successful speech delivery is to make sure that your speech is appropriate for the occasion (see previous chapter) and that you have rehearsed it properly.

Ending the speech

If done with care and patience, your speech will probably have mildly embarrassed the groom and entertained the guests. When it comes to ending your speech a favoured method is to raise the tone by praising the groom and his bride.

Spend thirty seconds or so highlighting the groom's best qualities and why these will be of benefit during his married years (e.g. is he loyal, hard-working, etc.) then end by raising your glass and toasting the bride and the groom by saying something like:

'To the bride and groom. May they enjoy a long life and happiness together.'

Depending on the nature of your speech and the wedding, it is possible that the groom or bride might want to offer an impromptu reply to your speech. However, your role is complete so you can sit back and enjoy the rest of the proceedings safe in the knowledge that you have done a good job.

Part Three
Social Occasions

The Guest Speaker
Speaking to Strangers

- How Not to Do It
- How You Fit In
- Structuring Your Speech
- Proposing a Toast
- Use of Notes
- Rehearsing
- Delivery and Communication

Speaking to an invited audience was once the preserve of the upper echelons of Victorian society who would lecture guests on weighty social or scientific subjects. More recently this tradition has been partially replaced by celebrities, comedians and former politicians who can charge exorbitant fees for delivering humorous or thought-provoking speeches at after-dinner and other functions. However, there are also smaller events at which a local person might be asked to deliver a talk about some aspect of their life or accomplishments.

Over the last few years local charities and societies have taken to organising dinners as a means of fund raising and so it is not inconceivable that you could be approached to be their guest speaker. Equally well, your boss could ask you to deliver a speech at the end of your company's annual dinner or, as the president or chair of a sports or social club, you might be expected to speak at an annual meeting. This could be a scary prospect but if you are properly prepared, then you can enjoy it.

How not to do it

I would like to begin by offering an example of how not to prepare and deliver a speech to an audience of strangers. I do this not to put you off but because I believe that it is often easier and quicker to learn best practice by examining the mistakes of others.

In June 2000 the then British Prime Minister and Labour party leader Tony Blair had been suffering from a bout of mid-term blues that affects many Westminster governments. On 7th June he stepped up to address 10,000 members of the Women's Institute (WI) at Wembley, London.

Blair was known as an orator with a particular flair for connecting with his audience. Often he did this by not sticking to his written script but instead choosing to relay a central message using his own words. On this occasion he did not.

Tony Blair had little input into the speech he was to deliver and instead relied upon his backroom staff to put together an appropriate message for the WI. However, the backroom staff misread the audience and assembled a speech that was overlong and overtly political. It also made several assumptions about the interests and demographic of the WI and kept stressing a belief in 'old fashioned values' perhaps in expectation that the audience was mostly middle class and older. Finally, by choosing to read his speech word for word from an autocue, Blair did not connect with his audience. He lacked sparkle and from the outset gave the appearance of being uncomfortable.

After only a few minutes his audience became restless and during the middle of his speech some people stood up and walked out. Then a section of the audience began a slow hand clap. There was a brief pause while the WI president appealed for calm but Blair was rattled and afterwards delivered the remainder of his (hastily shortened) speech in an uneasy, restless fashion.

In subsequent days the media made much mischief about the speech and in subsequent years it would be referred to by commentators and opposition MPs as an early sign that Labour's honeymoon with the British public was coming to an end. It need not have been like that.

In my opinion Blair went wrong that day because he broke several key rules associated with being a guest speaker. He delivered a speech which he had not written and with which he was unfamiliar. He did not understand his audience and did not pick up on, or react swiftly enough to their restlessness and so permitted it to develop into hostility.

Additionally, the speech was too long and on a subject that was inappropriate for the audience. Finally, he allowed himself to become flustered, at which point he lost the audience completely. We shall devote the rest of this section to ensuring that you avoid these and other pitfalls so that your after dinner speech will be both enjoyable and successful.

How you fit in

There is no set format for a dinner which has guest speakers. Smaller events, such as local charity or company dinners, will usually have a single guest speaker but at larger events there may be several speakers. It is therefore vital that you know what is expected of you and how you will fit into the general proceedings.

Your first requirement, therefore, is to get in touch with your host (or the person representing them) and ask them about the following points:

- What is the occasion and purpose of the dinner? Ask how much the tickets are and whether any profit will be going to charity. If you do not feel comfortable with the set up, then refuse the invitation to speak.

- Who are the audience? Try to discover something about their age and background. How many people are expected to attend?

- What is the purpose of your speech? Are you there to entertain or to inform? Are you expected to speak on a particular topic or do you have a free reign? To avoid any confusion or recriminations, give your host a title for your speech and a brief outline of its contents (this need only be a paragraph) so that they know what to expect.

- If your host wants you to deliver a speech that they have prepared then request a copy before agreeing to anything. Make sure that you have full licence to alter a set text so it can be tailored to your personality.

- Establish how long you are expected to speak. I do not recommend speaking for more than 30 to 40 minutes. Make sure that you and your host are in agreement about the length of the speech beforehand.

- Ask when you will be expected to speak. If possible request that you speak before about 10.30 pm. Any later than this and the audience may be restless, drunk or sleepy.

- What is the dress code? Both you and your audience will feel embarrassed if you arrive in evening dress when a more casual attire is appropriate (or vice versa).

- Where is the venue? How big is it and what are the acoustics and lighting like?

- Where will you be speaking? Will it be from your dinner place or on a stage, etc.? Will there be a microphone or lectern?

The answers to these few questions should give you a basic understanding of your venue and audience. You will need to have this information *before* you start writing your speech.

It also helps to have an understanding of the running order of the dinner and where you will be expected to be speaking.

Most dinners will be hosted by a chairman/woman who will welcome everyone at the beginning of the evening. They may also choose to introduce the top table guests and speakers before the meal so make sure that your hosts have an abbreviated biography which will allow them to introduce you using two or three sentences.

The dinner then follows and, after the dessert plates are cleared away and comfort breaks enjoyed, the chairman will set the scene for the evening's events. Sometimes you will be preceded by the chairman's speech or perhaps by a series of formal or informal toasts. Either way, you should stay seated until you are introduced to the audience, at which time you should get to your feet and/or move to the position from which you are to speak. Wait a moment for any subsequent clapping to die down and then the audience is all yours.

Structuring your speech

The secret of after dinner speaking is good preparation irrespective of what form the audience takes. No matter how experienced you are, or think you are, you cannot turn up at a venue with no preparation and expect to deliver a world-beating speech. Some after dinner speakers may claim to be able to speak entirely off the cuff but they are almost certainly lying. You must do the relevant research and preparation then write out a script of your speech which you can use to practice and rehearse.

All speeches should flow naturally from one point to the next and should be structured to have a beginning, middle and end.

The beginning will be brief and should give you an opportunity to introduce yourself and the theme of you speech. A good opening is essential. If you can make it snappy and humorous the audience will warm to you so give some thought to your opening few lines. A well-used and effective technique is to make a humorous reference to either your host, audience or venue; do this by undertaking some basic research on the Internet or in a library. Do not assume that you know your audience by the organisation to which they belong.

Mentioning your host or venue gives the audience a chance to laugh at themselves and lets them know that you have done your homework. As with all humour, make sure that it is appropriate to the occasion and always steer clear of risqué or offensive jokes.

The main thrust of your speech should be delivered in the middle section. Structure this carefully so that it meets the requirement of the evening. Most after dinner speakers are expected to use humour but do not try and be a stand up comedian. The audience would rather hear a few real life anecdotes which are amusing rather than listening to a string of inappropriate jokes gathered from the Internet. As with the beginning, try and introduce humour that refers to the audience whether they be insurers, bankers, architects, lawyers, golfers or footballers.

Above all, remember that you are there to entertain the audience, not yourself. Keep your jokes appropriate and do not make fun of anyone in the audience without first checking with them. Likewise, avoid politics and religion unless you are sure of your audience's affiliation.

Keep your speech tight. Choose a central theme and make sure that you return to it regularly. It helps if you have goal or purpose in mind and structure your speech so that it moves towards this. Do not be tempted to ramble and do not be afraid to keep the speech short; people rarely grumble if a speech is short but they will become restless or start to nod off if it is too long.

Unlike a business presentation, the end of your speech does not have to include a summary or conclusion of what has gone before. After dinner speeches often finish with a punchline or with a line or two that wraps up what has been said previously. At an amateur level many people end with a well-crafted line which makes it clear that the speech is finished and which is the equivalent of: 'and they all lived happily ever after.'

Make sure that your audience knows you have finished. Deliver your last line with a sense of purpose, pause briefly then say something like 'thank you and goodnight'. The audience will then know that you have finished and can start to applaud. Stand still during the applause but after a short while look towards the chairman and signal that you are finished. He or she will then take over the proceedings and you can return to your seat.

Proposing a toast

If you have been called upon to toast a society or organisation then it is important to get their name right. Check beforehand the correct title of the organisation and anyone you intend to mention by name. Write these on to a blank postcard and be prepared to read them out, if necessary.

As you reach the end of your speech, invite the audience to charge their glasses and stand. Wait for the noise to subside before calling out the toast itself.

The correct form is along the lines of:
'Ladies and gentlemen, please charge your glasses, stand and join me in the toast to XXXX Club and to its President Mr XXXX'

This makes it clear that everyone but the president should join the toast.

If you have been asked to propose a toast to the guests, then enquire in advance for the names of any people who should be specifically mentioned. Leave it to the host or chairman to decide who should and should not be mentioned by name as omissions can cause hurt feelings and you do not want to be responsible for any repercussions.

If you are replying on behalf of the guests, then you likely to be speaking after several other people so make sure that your toast is not too long and that it does not repeat what has been said already. If necessary you should prepare several versions so that you can pick the most suitable one on the night itself.

The use of notes

Unless you are a highly experienced public speaker, it is recommended you prepare your speech in full and then talk using cue cards or abbreviated notes. You do not have to stick to your speech verbatim but it is good for your nerves if you know that you have everything to hand.

If you elect to read from a script then it is recommended you use A4 sheets with a large, clear font at least 16 point and with double spaced lines. You can use highlighter pens to emphasise the start of paragraphs or particular phrases that you wish to deliver word perfect.

If the font is large enough then you should be able to read your notes from a behind a lectern (see below) by discreetly looking downwards. However, even if you elect to read your speech, make sure you rehearse it thoroughly so that you can deliver small parts of it from memory. This will stop the speech from sounding dry and mechanical and allows you to look up at the audience periodically.

If you have experience with public speaking then it may make more sense to use abbreviated notes or prompt cards. Notes can be handwritten or typed on blank postcards but they must be easily accessible and readable. Rather than write out your entire speech, it is better to use bullet points as an *aide mémoire* to guide you to your next prepared element. Bullet-pointed notes can be very effective if you have properly rehearsed your speech (see below) and are familiar with its contents. It allows you to look at your audience and utilise good eye contact as you will not be in danger of becoming note-bound.

If your host has indicated that you will be using a lectern then ask whether it has a lip. If so, then you will be able to rest your notes on the lectern which will leave your hands free.

If there is no lectern or it has no lip, then you will need to hold your notes in one hand, in which case postcards are probably more convenient as they are more portable, do not rustle and are less distracting than A4 sheets.

Whatever type of lectern you have, do not make your notes obvious by waving them about, by turning each page face down as you finish it or lifting it off the lectern and laying it on the table.

This can all be avoided if you number your note pages and start your speech by laying sheet one on the right of the lectern with sheet two alongside it to the left. As you get to the bottom of sheet one of your speech you are in a position to cast your eyes on to page two and continue speaking without hesitation as you slide page two over on top of page one revealing page three on the left. Careful sleight of hand during your speaking will enable you to move your notes discreetly from left to right when it best suits you without drawing too much attention to them.

When using notes of whatever kind, try not to read out jokes and anecdotes directly from the script as this tends make them sound dry and soulless. Instead rehearse it out loud repeatedly to ensure you get the content and punch line correct then put a key word in your notes to remind you of the story. If you are not sure enough of a joke or anecdote to tell it without having to read it, then it may be an idea to use other material instead.

And no matter how good a joke is, if it or something similar to it has already been used by an earlier speaker then abandon it. Do not be tempted to tell the same joke again and then apologise for doing so. It will not be any funnier the second time.

Rehearsing

Rehearsal is the key to success. At the very least it will familiarise you with the content of your speech but it should also allow you to fine tune its content and to make sure that it is not too long or rambling.

Practice by delivering your speech out loud. Do not worry about timing during the first couple of rehearsals as you will probably need to stop every now and then to change something in your notes. When you are happy with the speech as it stands, practice delivering it against the clock so that you have a rough idea of its length. Make allowances for any audience laughter but bear in mind that whatever time your rehearsal takes will almost certainly be an under-estimate. On the day itself you will take longer (by as much as 10 to 20 per cent) so make allowances for this.

When rehearsing be aware of other possible interferences with your carefully prepared speech. On the day itself you may find a previous speaker has used one or more of your jokes so you should prepare a fallback position. Equally well, you may hear something said during dinner or mentioned by a previous speaker which you can make good use of in your speech. Be prepared to make minor alterations to your speech on the day but do not be tempted to do a major rewrite. If you have rehearsed sufficiently then you will know your prepared material well enough to allow for the addition of some more minor jokes.

Delivery and communication

On the big day you should take the opportunity to check the room and familiarise yourself with all the facilities. Check the room's layout, lighting, lectern and ask whether the microphone is a clip-on, handheld or attached to the lectern. Find out where you will be sitting and from where you will be speaking. Use this information to decide where your notes will be and how best you can address the audience so that you are audible and visible.

In order to be successful your speech needs to be heard. If you have a microphone then you do not need to worry too much. However, you should still speak clearly into a microphone but do not be tempted to shout or speak directly into it. Hold it (or position it) below your mouth and speak over the its top.

If you are speaking without a microphone then ensure you speak clearly and loudly and that your words are directed towards the back of the room.

If it is a big venue then get someone to check that you can be heard from the back but bear in mind that an empty room provides different acoustics to a one full. If necessary, at the beginning of your speech, ask people at the back if they can hear you (this can be a good technique for getting the audience on your side).

Make a point of directing your delivery to all corners of the room. Eye contact is often mentioned but this can be misleading. With a small audience you can make eye contact with individuals although it is probably safer to look at the foreheads of individuals. They will still think you have looked at them and you will not get too distracted by catching someone's eye.

With a large audience all you are required to do is scan the room as you speak by turning your head and body from side to side and cover all corners, sides and centre of the room. Remember all this has to be achieved whilst still maintaining good connection with your notes.

If your microphone breaks down then this is a problem for the chairman to resolve. He may seek help from a technician or he may get a new microphone provided. However, if you have to carry on without one, in which case speak slowly and loudly.

Before speaking do not eat too much and avoid all alcohol. Even a small amount of drink will affect your concentration and memory while anything more could result in slurred speech and an inability to follow your own notes.

Much can depend on where your position is in the speaking order and when you come on. If you are down the pecking order, the performance of earlier speakers can influence how receptive your audience will be. If the previous speakers are good then the audience will be feeling good and happy to give you plenty of rope.

If the previous speakers are poor performers then this can work in your favour because, if you are better than them, then the audience will be delighted that the evening is improving. As has been said before, do not be frightened to adapt or alter aspects of your speech if you think it will make for a better or more relevant performance.

Finally, most dinners are accompanied by a liberal amount of alcohol and this can lead to a certain degree of exuberance on the part of the audience. Heckling or poor behaviour (such as food throwing) can be a possibility, especially at annual dinners of sports clubs, birthdays, school reunions, etc. Minor heckling can usually be ignored but in the case of serious rowdiness (e.g. persistent vocal shouting) you should stop and wait for the chairman (or some other official) to step in. Do not get spooked but stand still and, with head held high, stare at your audience until they are quiet. Then carry on as if nothing had happened. If the situation becomes intolerable (e.g. food is being thrown at you) then you are within your rights to abandon speaking altogether. It is up to your hosts to provide you with a safe platform from which to deliver your speech.

That said, I have never had to abandon a speech. On the contrary, I have found the experience of talking to an audience enjoyable and rewarding and I expect that you will too.

Friends and Family
Informal Speaking at Family Gatherings

This section acts as an addendum to Chapter 10 and will give you some hints should you ever need to make an informal speech where the subject of the talk is a friend or family member.

Over the years I have been called upon on many occasions to speak in public, either at professional meetings or more latterly at lunch clubs or after dinner. Techniques for capturing the attention of one's audience, and keeping them involved, have changed markedly in recent years; so has the technology. However, although we are now light years away from the days when I would stand up and speak using with a few notes and prompts, I am relieved to say that the basic principles remain the same.

There are many occasions when one may be asked to give a speech about a friend or family member. It might be their birthday or retirement. They may be about to emigrate or even have received an award or trophy. Whatever the cause, it is important to get the mood and tone right, especially if the subject of your speech is also in the room. As with best man speeches (see Chapters 8 and 9), it is all too easy to offend your audience or to make a speech that is incoherent or rambling.

Unlike after dinner speaking to strangers, the central advantage of addressing friends and family is that you will know many of the people present and they will know you. This is important because most after dinner speeches about friends will ideally involve a mixture of humour and praise and it is essential to get the right balance of both.

Even if you know everyone, it pays to gauge the age, sex and attitude of the audience so that you can keep any quips at the right level. Do not aim your humour exclusively at a certain section of your audience, but to everyone. Excessive crudity in the wrong company reflects badly on the speaker and therefore also on the subject of your speech. However, the use of a clever joke at the start of your talk can be effective and may even revive the attention of flagging audience members.

An in-joke is always a good attention-getter. However, I have heard a number of jokes that are so 'in' and obscure that they go over most people's heads and therefore fail to break the ice. This situation is unnecessary and can be avoided with a little prior research amongst the other attendees. A relevant introductory joke or anecdote can get the audience on-side and keep them there until the next point of interest.

Avoid manufactured jokes (especially one liners) as these are hard to carry off and will more than likely fall flat. Instead, take a tip from the most accomplished alternative comedians who rely on story-telling rather than wise cracks to entertain their audience. You should arm yourself with some good stories but explain them properly and do not assume that everyone knows the context.

Comedy should only be part of your routine. The usual aim of an after dinner speech to friends is in some way to pay tribute to an individual. Make sure that you know enough details about the occasion and balance the praise and comedy according to the individual concerned.

Try to build your speech up towards a finale; especially if the subject of your talk has achieved something, such as an award. It is possible that there may be the award of a trophy or gift which may require the introduction of a third party. If so then make sure that this becomes a seamless part of the speech and be prepared to thank the third party carefully afterwards.

Use such physical aids as you need to produce a smooth flowing speech. There is nothing worse than silence when you are grasping for your next line. Equally the rote memorising of a speech can lead to a wooden and insincere delivery which can easily be derailed by a misplaced laugh or interruption. Similarly, reading a speech can be dull and monotonous as our reading voices are not our natural speaking voices and carry little light and shade.

The best speakers, as with the best stand up comedians, structure their talks around loose headings and only memorise topics, not whole routines. One of the funniest speakers I have heard kept a long roll of paper in his pocket, supposedly with his speech or some nice things to say about the subject. He then contrasted this with a tiny piece of paper listing the 'good points' of his friend. If there is an object of particular relevance, keep it hidden until the appropriate time and make sure you can reveal it smoothly, without clumsiness and quickly to ensure maximum impact.

I mentioned earlier that technology has developed apace over the last twenty years and it is now permissible to bring a small laptop or tablet computer into an after dinner speech. One word of caution. Make sure it works. Do not rely on unfamiliar technology which can let you down, and realise that it is not a substitute for practice. Rehearsing one's speech to friends or family is still the best way to appear relaxed and fluent. Certainly, being unable to boot up a laptop and then not being able to find the relevant presentation is no more impressive in a social situation than in it is in a business presentation. There are ways to avoid this and once again it involves repetition of both the speech and the process of setting up well in advance until they become second nature.

A word of warning though. However good one's speech, and however slick one's set up, this is not an excuse for addressing an audience with eyes and face downcast toward the screen. This is no better than reading it off a piece of paper and is, in fact, likely to be worse as you will have to keep scrolling down the screen when reading.

A far more entertaining method of after-dinner speech using new technology is to involve a computer-generated slide presentation. This enables you to combine public domain images with personal images to maximum effect. A little skulduggery helps and obtaining pictures from the subjects' friends prior to the speech and scanning them in to a laptop makes for an amusing and memorable evening. Contributors will also have the satisfaction of knowing they helped to make it a success and have contributed to the subject's pleasure.

Needless to say any pictures should not be risqué and should never be offensive. More than ever it is important to master the technology required to make this work well and it is therefore essential that you make sure that the computers or other equipment you need are available and will work at your venue.

I have delivered a talk to a social club where I was told that a laptop projector was available. However, when I got to the venue the projector was not compatible with my laptop. Having loaded my talk onto a memory stick and located a compatible laptop, I then found that the projector was broken. In short, using computers is a risky gambit but if it pays off, then the rewards can be great indeed. As well as giving the audience something other to look at, slides will also act as an *aide mémoire* to the speaker. Certainly the best after dinner speeches I have attended in recent years have been accompanied by a slide show.

Do not make your speech too long. Twenty minutes to half an hour is more than enough and many are far shorter than this. Lastly, do not forget why you are there. Someone, somewhere along the line thought you were the right person for the job and you therefore owe them the courtesy of doing your best. You never know, this may be the beginning of a new career in after-dinner speaking.

The Anniversary Speech
How to Write One at Short Notice

Imagine the situation. You have been invited to a close friend's surprise birthday party but that morning the host/hostess rings up and asks if you would 'say a few words' to mark the occasion. You do not really have the time to prepare anything but fortunately the informal and celebratory nature of the occasion means that you do not need to spend hours or days preparing an elaborate speech. A few well-chosen words delivered in a relaxed, informal manner should suffice.

Anniversary parties (especially surprise ones) are generally informal and joyous occasions which gather together people who are familiar with each other (e.g. friends and family) and at which food and alcoholic drink are liberally provided. At some point during the proceedings there is often a call for silence so that a presentation, such as a birthday cake, presents or award, can be produced and/or the birthday song can be sung. It is usually at this time that a few words can be given by a speaker as a means of gaining the crowd's attention and of flattering the person whose anniversary it is.

At such informal occasions, the speaker will not be the focus of attention and, unless you are told otherwise, there should be no need to create an elaborate best man style speech. (NB If you have been asked to provide a full speech then consult the best man section in this book as the format and content required are very similar.)

Instead your task should be relatively simple. At a prescribed moment you will need to interrupt the celebration, gain the full attention of the guests and then introduce the anniversary boy or girl using a speech that will last no more than a few minutes.

Interrupt the proceedings

Interrupting a party in full swing is a matter of self-confidence. The venue (be it a garden BBQ, parish hall or restaurant) is likely to be noisy and crowded so you will need to be able to make yourself seen and heard.

If everyone is sitting down at tables then stand up and use your hands to gesture gently for silence. As the noise begins to dies down try raising your voice and repeating a phrase such as:

'Ladies and gentlemen, may I please have your attention...'

This will eventually gain you the silence and attention you need. Alternatively get a friend or the party's host to interrupt the proceedings on your behalf. Hitting the side of a glass gently with a knife or fork can work but it brings the risk of showering your neighbours with broken glass.

If the party is informal and everyone is standing around, then you will need to find a suitable part of the room from which you can be seen and heard. It is better to have your entire audience in front of you, rather than them surrounding you on all sides as this makes it easier for you to project your voice and for others to hear you. The front of a room or a convenient corner can suffice; if there is a stage or some other device that can lift you above the height of the crowd, then so much the better. In an emergency you could try standing on a chair but make sure it is sturdy and secure before doing so.

The speech

Your speech should last no longer than a few minutes (five at most) and, as with most speeches, it should be divided into three parts: an introduction; a middle; and an end.

The introduction

This needs to be short and to acknowledge:
- The person whose anniversary it is.
- The hosts/people that organised the party.
- Those attending the party.

You should be able to do this in a short paragraph which might read as follows:

'Ladies and gentlemen. On behalf of **[hosts' names]** it is my pleasure to welcome you here today/tonight in celebration of XXXX's XXth birthday. We are delighted to have so many friends and relations with us on such a special occasion and we thank you for taking the trouble to be here tonight, especially if you have had to travel from afar. Before we [eat/cut the cake/etc.] I have been asked to say a few words about XXXX.'

The middle

The middle part of your speech should contain a few select remarks or observations about the person's anniversary. As with most public speeches, do not be tempted to tell offensive stories and/or reveal secrets or events which might upset members of the audience. People attending a private party often know the person concerned in different contexts (e.g. through work or a hobby, as a relative or neighbour, etc.). Make sure that what you say will not radically alter people's opinion of the host. Keep it humorous, positive and light-hearted.

Stick to the tried and tested themes of informal speeches which generally concern the person's age, occupation and hobbies. Below is a list of some commonly used ideas that utilise these themes: pick two or three of these and make them applicable to the person.

- Work out the year in which they were born and find some famous event, such as a the moon landing, that will allow you to put the person's age in context.

- Work out the week in which they were born and find some music that was in the charts at this time. The Internet or a local library should be able to help you.

- Where was the person living when they born? How does this relate to where they are now.

- Does the person have a hobby or interest for which they are well-known? Do they play in a team or are they a member of a golf club, etc.?

- What is their occupation? Is it unusual or noteworthy (a lumberjack, lifeguard, etc.)? If it is a regular job, then are there any stereotypical (but clean) jokes that can safely be made about it (e.g. accountants are often thought to be rather straight-laced)?

- Speak with the family to find out what the person was like as a child or as a teenager. What job did they want when they grew up (astronaut, train driver)? What interests did they have then? What car did they drive? What music did they listen to and did they wear any distinctive clothes/hairstyle to go with it (e.g. were they a punk, hippie, rocker, etc.)? Compare it with now.

- Is it a milestone anniversary such as a 21st, 40th or 60th? There is milage in the idea of moving from youth to middle or middle to old age, etc. However, not everyone appreciates having attention drawn to their age, so be aware. Also be aware of mentioning impending death, even if it is in jest: it probably will not bother someone who is in their thirties but it might not go down well if they are in their eighties.

- Look for some useful quotes on the Internet regarding age and anniversaries and perhaps to choose one or two that you have not already heard a hundred times before.

- Is there any forthcoming event or occasion which you could mention? For example, a planned house move, change of career, etc.

- Does the person have any well-known characteristics or traits which you can mention without causing offence? Do they tell corny jokes? Are they always late/early for everything? Are they laid back or constantly on the go?

You are probably looking for no more than three or four short paragraphs for the middle section of your speech, so do not be tempted to include everything. Essentially you are trying to place the person's anniversary (and possibly age) in context by looking at their past and present life. It ought to be possible to do this in only a few minutes.

The Conclusion

This wraps up the speech succinctly and lets the audience know that you are finished and that they can get back to the party. As with the introduction, you need to keep the conclusion short and simple. Finish by offering a compliment to the person whose anniversary it is and by offering a toast in their favour. It might run something like this:

'It goes without saying, but I will say it anyway, that XXXX is a generous warm-hearted person who means so much to everybody here. Let's raise our glasses in a birthday toast to XXXX. Here's to XXXX and another XX happy and productive years. Happy [birthday/anniversary]!'

Writing a Eulogy
Saying Farewell to a Loved One

- Creating a Structure
- A List of Helpful Hints

Most social gatherings take the form of a celebration but there are more sombre occasions where people are required to make speeches. The most commonly encountered of these is at a funeral or commemorative service where it is traditional for a close friend or family member to say a few words on behalf of the departed in the form of a eulogy.

Writing and delivering a eulogy is rarely an easy task. The passing of a friend or relation can be a traumatic experience and the process of organising a funeral can be emotionally draining and time consuming. Finding the time and frame of mind to sit down and put together a meaningful speech about the deceased's life can problematic. Nonetheless, while the process of assembling a eulogy might be an unwanted duty, it does offer you an opportunity to laud the life and accomplishments of a loved one and to give others an insight into your thoughts and feelings.

If you have agreed to give a eulogy then I suggest finding a quiet area or location where you are unlikely to be disturbed for at least couple of hours. Once there, settle down and gather your thoughts together.

A good tip is to try not to think about the death of the person but instead focus on the person that they were during life. In particular, think about their achievements, their relationships with other people and those behavioural characteristics and habits that helped define who they were. As thoughts and memories come into your head, note them down and, when you are ready, set about organising your notes into a coherent order.

Creating a structure

Eulogies are much like any other speech in that they are required to have an introduction, a middle and an end. A eulogy consisting of random thoughts and memories can work, but they tend to be the exception rather than the rule.

The introduction to a eulogy is usually brief and in many cases may only consist of a few words of explanation as to who you are and what your relationship is to the deceased. This is especially important if this relationship is not immediately obvious and/or not known to all those attending the funeral. It is a way of letting the guests know why you are qualified to speak on the subject of the deceased person's life.

Unlike wedding speeches, the introduction to a eulogy does not require you to reel off a long list of thank-yous to those involved in the organisation of the funeral. These are often best done in private after the service.

The middle section of a eulogy is its main part and should focus on the deceased person's life and their relationship to family and friends. A suggested outline of the eulogy's content is discussed below but in general this part should be upbeat and positive (and even occasionally amusing), accentuating the person's life and accomplishments. You should mention those people who were most dear to the deceased (close friends and family) but do not feel obliged to include every single person attending the funeral.

Summarising a person's life into a few minutes is no easy task. So, instead of trying to fit everything in to one speech, you should create a list of the deceased's most memorable achievements as well as a list of events and personality traits for which they were well-known. These might include information on:

- The person's age.
- Their family, friends and relationships.
- Their upbringing, education and work.
- Their hobbies and personal achievements.
- Any places or objects (e.g. a favourite car) which people associate with them.

Once you have a list of items you want to include, try organising them into a coherent order. Many eulogies begin chronologically by describing the person's birth and upbringing before moving onto education, early career and marriage. After this may come a more general recollection of the deceased's life including their hobbies, close relations, personality characteristics and hopes and ambitions. This is a logical means of proceeding which is easy to follow.

Rather than producing a speech that becomes a list of dates and names, try to attach anecdotes to some of the important events in the person's life. These might illustrate aspects of the person's character (e.g. were they so determined to get a particular job that they applied for it seven or eight times?), their history or their relationships with other people.

This may sound odd, but consider including some humour in your eulogy. Funerals might be a sad occasions but they are not supposed to be depressing. It is entirely appropriate to recall funny anecdotes and the opportunity to smile or laugh will be appreciated by others. However, laugh out loud humour is best used sparingly in a eulogy and it is better to make people smile or chuckle rather than guffaw.

Do not be frightened to personalise the eulogy. You will have memories which others may not be aware of and it is appropriate for you to describe the deceased person from your perspective. However, make sure that you do not hog the limelight or exclude other important people from the eulogy as this can cause immense offence.

The eulogy's conclusion is usually brief. It can be sombre and reflective, reminding the funeral guests why they are at a funeral. As such it often stands in contrast to the more positive, reminiscent tone of the middle section.

Typically a conclusion will say something about the person's final months/years and, if appropriate, something of the manner of their death (e.g. they fought bravely against an illness, it was sudden and unexpected, etc.).

The conclusion may also provide reasons as to why the person should be remembered by the guests as well as future generations. As with the introduction, there is no need to end with a long list of thank yous. It is entirely appropriate to finish your piece and then to sit down again afterwards.

A list of helpful hints

- Write the eulogy ahead of time and practice it.

- Keep the eulogy short. Five minutes should be plenty.

- Consult with family and friends before delivering the speech, especially if you are unsure about aspects of your eulogy's content. Do not be frightened to discuss the eulogy with other people, including any priest or religious person conducting the service. They will have heard dozens of eulogies and may have some useful advice.

- The following questions will help you construct your eulogy:

    - How close were you to them?

    - What did you learn from their life?

    - What were their principles in life?

    - What made them happy?

    - What were the pleasant moments shared with the person?

    - What aspects of the person's personality were captivating?

    - What did family and friends think of them?

    - What would they like to be remembered for?

    - What words of solace can you give to the family left behind?

- With most speeches it is better to use cue cards rather than reading the speech verbatim. However, the emotion and trauma of delivering a eulogy means that reading from a script is perfectly appropriate. Even so, it will help to practice it out loud several times before the funeral.

- If delivering the eulogy is liable to be a highly emotional affair then it may be an idea to arrange for someone who could stand in for you, should the occasion become too much.

- Speak slowly and clearly. Pause to gather your composure if necessary and do not be frightened to cry.

- Do not be overly influenced by eulogies that have been delivered at famous funerals or on film/television programmes.

Part Four
Charity Events

The Charity Auction
Organising and Hosting your own Auction

- Which Type of Auction?
- Acquiring the Lots
- Equipment
- The Auctioneer
- Humour
- Momentum
- Upping the Ante
- Closing the Bid
- Sweeping Up

We have probably all been to a charity auction – even if we did not mean to. I have been to several dinner dances and cheese and wine evenings where, midway through the evening, silence is called for and an auctioneer (sometimes of dubious quality) tries to drum up some extra cash for which ever charity event you happen to be at.

Most such events are organised and hosted as amateur events and as such the auction can be the highlight of the evening. Or it can be a cringe-worthy fiasco. Hopefully, with the help of this short guide, if you are about to host a charity auction you will not fall into the second category!

Which type of auction?

Before embarking on any organised event where you are expected to speak, remember the rule of the 'six Ps':

Proper Preparation and Planning Prevents Poor Performance

If you try to host an event without a coherent and thought out plan then you will fall on your face (unless you are monumentally lucky).

Your first task is to decide on which type of auction you want. There are four main types:

- Online auction
- Silent auction
- Dutch auction
- Traditional auction

The first two do not require any real speech making and so I will describe them briefly.

Online auctions

As the name implies these auctions are held via the Internet – either over a matter of days or even weeks. Think of eBay and you realise how popular online auctions have become. You can host a charity auction in a similar way – and in fact some online auction sites (including eBay) have a dedicated charity auction system which tells people how much of their bid will go to charity. The attraction of this is that the online auctioneer will automatically send the money to the charity so the bidder knows that their money will end up in the right hands. For more details of online auctions visit one of the online auction sites and see their terms and conditions.

Silent auctions

Unlike online auctions, a silent auction is attached to a real event (such as charity dinner) but it runs in the background and so does not take much time out of the evening. All silent auctions begin with a printed list of lots that is either handed to each guest as they arrive or placed on their table.

Following this the auction can be organised in a couple of ways.

Version one works by putting on each table (and by the lots themselves) a pile of bidding slips on which the bidder puts their name, telephone number, the lot number they are bidding for and their bid. The completed slips are either handed to volunteers or posted into slotted boxes by each lot. (The boxes do not have to be fancy – a shoe box wrapped in glitzy paper will do.) At the end of the evening the volunteers check the slips, work out who posted the highest bid and announce the winner. The drawback to this is that people are effectively submitting sealed bids which prevents the atmosphere of friendly (and not so friendly!) rivalry that can develop in more open situations.

Version two is to get bidders to write their name and bid on a piece of paper next to the lot. This allows people to see how much someone else has bid and so gives them an opportunity to raise their bid (thus it is a little like an online auction where you know what the current highest bid is). Make sure people know when the bidding will close and, if possible, arrange for a clock to countdown towards this moment. Doubtless you will see people popping up to the lots with a minute to go to make their final bid and then trying to hog the list to prevent others from bidding!

An even better technique (if you have the equipment) is to display a real time list of the maximum bid on each lot but you'll need an alert volunteer to keep it updated. In the past flip boards and over head projectors were useful for this task but nowadays laptops linked to projectors are a good option. This also makes it quicker and easier to announce the winners as the information has been updated throughout the evening.

Dutch auction

This is where the auctioneer starts with a high price and then reduces it gradually as time passes. The first person to make a bid wins the lot. These auctions are great fun – there's a real element of brinksmanship as potential bidders try to hold out for as long as possible without losing the lot.

Dutch auctions were originally designed to sell tulips in Holland and so work very quickly. You would normally expect to reduce the price by about 70 per cent within the first minute so bear this in mind when deciding on the opening amount. This style of auction is designed to be fast and furious and can be ideal if you have a large amount of lots to get through. However, you will need quick reactions to spot the first bid and having extra spotters (a bit like baseline judges in tennis) can rule out any arguments as to who put their hand up first.

Traditional auctions

Most people will be familiar with this style of auction, even if it is only through watching them on television. The auctioneer begins with a low price and invites the audience to offer continually higher bids. When there are no further bids, the last bidder wins that lot.

These are the basic auction types. Online and silent auctions do not require much input from the auctioneer and will not be discussed any further here. The other two auctions I shall talk about in greater detail in a short while, but first I want to say something on how to go about organising an auction in the first place.

Acquiring the lots

It is possible that if you are hosting the auction then you may also be involved in organising it. If so, then you will need to find a means of sourcing some decent lots at a low cost (or preferably free).

The time honoured way to get items for a charity auction is to ask for donations from local businesses and organisations. Make sure you do your homework and find out the best person to contact and then phone or write to them personally. A letter addressed to "Dear Sir/Madam" will often end up in the bin; the personalised touch is a better route. Explain who you are and what the funds from the auctions are being used for. Keep the letter short and, if there is no reply, do not be afraid to send a follow up letter or make a phone call. Be persistent but polite and if it is clear that the business is not interested, then simply thank them and move on.

Make sure that you target the right businesses. If your charity involves a children's sports club, then ask sports shops or local sports clubs. If it is an animal welfare charity then try pet shops, riding stables, etc. Make sure the businesses know that their name will feature prominently in the auction literature and/or any advertising associated with the event. Invite them along, but make sure they buy a ticket! If you are hosting a high end event then think about having some corporate tables so that they can impress clients or business rivals.

Take advantage of local networks. Can your colleagues and friends ask their contacts to donate an item. Do not limit yourself to trying to obtain physical objects from high street shops - ask people if they have a skill or service they could offer for auction. It is common for charity auctions to offer guided walks, pony rides, etc., offered by members of the public as well as other more formal experiences such as hot air ballooning and glider flying.

Remember that you will only have a limited time to hold your auction so you need good quality, high interest auction lots. Auctioning off dozens of low value items usually does not generate much money and can be tedious. It is sometimes better to offer smaller items as secondary prizes in a raffle as they can generate more money this way.

Advertise

The auction is usually one part of a larger event (such as dinner) so it may not be the central attraction. Nonetheless make sure that it features prominently in your leaflets, press adds, website and newsletters, etc., and that any businesses that have been promised advertising are in there as well. Place adverts anywhere people will see them - posters in windows, leaflets by tills, on websites, banners on railings - anywhere (so long as it is legal; do not get hauled in for fly-posting).

Equipment

If you are using a PA or radio mike then make sure that the thing works. Check that volume is correct and that it is not going to screech with feedback as soon as you speak. Having to speak loudly or shout is not a good option unless you are in a small venue.

Have a hammer and a block of wood – people will expect it and will like the sound of you closing the bid with a solid thump. It also gives you something to do with your hands and to point at people with.

Have at least one assistant to help spot bidders and record the amount and winner for each lot. Do not entrust this job to someone who is not organised and reliable. They have to get it right or you will be on the receiving end of some very vocal complaints. Having an assistant to do the paperwork allows you to be move on to the next lot quickly and so keeps momentum in the auction.

If you are holding the auction 'in the round' (i.e. in the centre of the audience) then have two assistants to spot for you. If you do not, you will end up spinning round like a boat in a whirlpool and will get dizzy.

So on to the real skill of a charity auction...

The auctioneer

If you've been asked to be the auctioneer you will fall into one of four categories.

- A professional auctioneer who's been asked to help out
- You've been 'press ganged' on the night
- You are a celebrity whose mere presence will ensure a good turn out for the event
- You've been approached by the event organiser ahead of the event as they think you'll make a good auctioneer. (Which is why you are reading this.)

Assuming that you have been asked ahead of time, then you should be flattered. Auctioneers are showmen who can control an audience with confidence and humour and you will need to become a natural salesman to generate as much money as possible, armed only with a microphone and a quick wit.

If this is not you, then now is the time to develop an alter ego. We have all seen them – the shy office junior who will not say a word but hand them a microphone and a karaoke machine and suddenly they become Tom Jones. Remember the role of the auctioneer is really an act: to talk up interest in the lots and ensure they sell. This gives you licence to be a little outrageous.

The key part of your act as an auctioneer is to know your lots!

Obtain a list of the lots before the evening and ask for any details of what they involve. If necessary then do some research on the Internet. If you are auctioning a meal for two then check to see if the restaurant specialises in a particular cuisine or even whether it has a Michelin star. If the lot is a ride in a performance car round a race track, then find out how fast the car goes. If you can give a colourful and enticing description of the item before you start the bidding, you will increase the number of bids and the amount raised.

Try to impart a mental picture of what the winner will get. I once raised a large sum of money with a glider flight by describing the beauty of swooping like a bird on a perfect summer day, watching the fields and towns below with only the wind to be heard, and that for some it was a life changing experience. It must have hit a chord with time poor, stressed executives who made up the audience because I was met with a forest of hands when the bidding opened.

Some things cannot be described in an emotional and evocative way – so you have to talk up their good points, perhaps with a bit of humour. For instance, I once had a lot that was a cordless drill – not exactly exciting – but after some research I knew how much it cost in the shops, how the trade rated it, how long the battery lasted, etc. So I introduced it as a lot I would like to bid on myself because of its high performance and good trade reviews – except as I had three cordless drills already and my wife was in the audience I was banned from buying anymore! It raised a laugh and sold well. (And, sadly, I really do have three cordless drills already.)

However, do not list every little detail of a lot – give the audience a taste, but not all the ingredients! If you lose people's interest it is hard to get it back.

If an item has been donated by a local business or individual then give them a name check. Always do a general thank you to all those who have donated to the auction and remind the audience of the charity and the good work it does. But keep it short.

Once you know your lots a bidding order will normally present itself. As a rule keep the star item until last as it will hold people's interest until the end. Have a high end item near the start (second or third lot) as the higher bids will help the audience to get a feel for the sort of money that is expected to be bid. Make a printed list of the bidding order and if you are using a helper to display items make sure they have a copy so that they are selecting the lots quickly. The list will also be used to record the winning bids.

Humour

To joke or not to joke... that is the question. Jokes make people laugh and that relaxes them. If they are relaxed they' bid more readily.

If you are good at telling jokes then feel free to do so but make sure they are appropriate and do not make the auction second fiddle to your comedy performance. If you want to know if you are good at telling jokes ask your friends. If you are not completely sure then leave jokes well alone – the silence that follows a failed wisecrack is uncomfortable and embarrassing.

If you want to avoid out right joke telling try some gentle auction-based anecdotes. These can be used to break up the auction if it is lengthy or if the bidders have gone quiet. Below are two examples I have used (with varying degrees of success):

> "I asked an auctioneer what skills he needed to do his job – he replied 'Lots!'"
> "I asked how much knowledge of the items I would need – he replied 'Lots!'"
> "I asked how much he earned – he replied 'Lots!'"
> "I asked him if he needed a good vocabulary – he replied 'No!'"

> "An auctioneer stops the auction and announces that a wallet containing £500 has been dropped and there is a £100 reward for its return. After a few moments silence a voice from the back shouts out '£101!'"

Momentum

The auction should be kept going at a brisk pace so that the audience gains a sense of urgency. If you wait too long for a final bid that never comes, then you begin to look desperate. Going slowly also sends the wrong message to the audience and gives them the impression that they have plenty of time to bid. You want hands to go up quickly – almost impulsively – and that does not happen if the pace is too slow.

Having said that do not bring the hammer down too soon. If you've only had two bids then give a bit more information out about the lot to fill the gap. If no one bites then sell and move on.

I have found a great way to inject momentum from the offset is to auction off something that is cheap and whose value is well-known. A famous New York auctioneer used to auction off a sandwich.... usually for less than it cost so if you were not quick you missed it.

You could try the same with a pint of beer or bottle of wine – and it allows you to remind the audience that this is a charity auction. They know the bottle is only worth £5 but may bid £10 as it is a cheap way for them to show their charitable nature to their friends, family, clients or colleagues.

A particularly successful technique is to begin by auctioning a lottery ticket. Everyone knows it is only worth £1, but it holds the chance of great wealth and I have had people bid £5 for it. Start at 10p and up the bids in small amounts as you want to get people around the room involved in the bidding. it is a bit of fun and not serious money but it gets people into the right frame of mind.

Upping the ante

Once the bidding starts you will quickly spot people whose hands go up a lot – they are either trying to impress or have a rivalry with someone in the room. (That or they are drunk and will regret their actions in the morning!) Let their competitive nature run its course. It helps to highlight these people (and if one of your helpers can put names to them even better) Flattering references such as "Ah, the big boys are bidding now", or "It's a fight to see which of the prettiest ladies will win this", will spur them on.

If you have a name and they stop bidding you can push them further with a well placed "Come on Mr. Smith, we all know you've got the money"; or "Are you sure you want to let this one go Bob – think of what so and so will think."

Remember this is a charity auction. – Be prepared to hammer that point home if the audience are being tight with their bids. Have details of the charity to hand to remind the audience what their money will go towards. Sounds simple but if you have several bidders all after the same lot then the bids will be firing in very quickly. Ensure you make it absolutely clear what the current top bid is – and this is one time when repetition is not only needed but is expected. So you should find yourself saying things like:

"£500 is the top bid. £500 over here to my left. £500. Do I hear more? £500, do I hear £525? £525 anyone? £500 it stands at - anyone for anymore? £525! Thank you sir! £525 is the bid to my right, £525. Do I hear any more?"

I am sure every other chapter in this book stresses the need to slow down when public speaking. If so then I have good news – for an auction, speed is your friend! By keeping up a torrent of commentary the auction keeps its pace and that means more bids.

Closing the bid and sweeping up

Possibly the most satisfying moment is when you ask: "Going once? Going twice? [suitable pause] Sold!"

Congratulate the winner. If the bidding has been particularly tense and a high figure achieved then ask the winner to stand up and the audience to give them a round of applause whilst praising the winner for their generosity. If you can, let the audience know the total raised at the end of the auction and thank them for their generosity.

Make sure the winners have paid up. Your assistants should have been getting cheques/cash/promissory notes during the evening. Check that the funds have been passed onto the event organiser.

And that's that! Happy auctioneering!

Closing the bid and closing down

The Charity Appeal
Speaking at a Fund Raising Event

- Preparing the Speech
- An Example Speech
- Some Things to Note

Small charities usually operate under financial pressure and often do not have the resources to employ professional fund raisers, advertise or organise large fund raising events. Instead they often rely on local initiatives which will bring in a steady trickles of cash throughout the year.

A time honoured means of fund raising is to organise an appeal, either for general funds or for a specific cause (such as new church roof). Associated with these will be events such as fairs, cake sales, etc., during which it may be necessary to give a small speech that explains the nature of the appeal and the associated charity. It is unlikely that the charity will have the resources of professional speech writers to assist them, so this section offers some guidance to assembling a fund raising speech by asking some basic questions.

What is the time available?
Timing is crucial in any speech. The time available for your speech is likely to be reasonably short, about five to ten minutes. Even if time is not restricted, your listener's attention will be. There usually will not be time for a lot of facts or detailed anecdotes. Be sure to bear that in mind when considering the whole content of your speech.

What is the setting for your speech and the limitations of the venue?
What is the size of your venue? How will you be heard? Will a microphone be available for a larger room or will the space be more intimate? Have you practiced in a venue like this? If not, will you have an opportunity to set up and test your venue in advance?

Will you have any other audio-visual aids and will they improve your communication or complicate it? Many people virtually read their audio-visual presentation from a screen they are showing their listeners. Whilst this might be good when delivering a lecture, it may hinder you reaching the hearts, minds and pockets of your listeners.

How will you be introduced?
First impressions will make many people decide whether it is worth listening before you even open your mouth. Of course you will want to dress appropriately, but also consider writing the blurb for the person introducing you. it is a bit like marketing yourself before you have to perform.

What does your audience expect?
What do you know about your audience? Speak to the organisers about who is liable to be attending the event and then create a mental picture of a typical person in your audience. What would you be expecting if you were in their shoes?

Most often your listeners will expect that your speech will be short. They are also not likely to be geared up to concentrate on what you have to say, so keep your sentences short and your language simple. Avoid jargon and acronyms. Their minds will drift if your speech is long or complicated.

If you do use visual aids then keep them simple and use as few as possible. Perhaps one or two to help support the picture you want your speech to build in their mind.

Will there be any audience interaction?

Consider whether your audience will want to ask any questions. Most charity appeals are straightforward speeches which do not make allowances for questions. However, if questions or a right to reply is thought desirable then be sure that your preparation is thorough enough to deal them. A poor response to a question will leave your listeners in doubt.

Preparing the speech

How will you gain your listeners' attention?

This is very important as you will probably have less than a minute to grab their attention. A good way to reach your listeners' hearts is by opening with a story that demonstrates how personal your charity work is to you and how close it is to your audience.

If you want an example of how to open your speech then listen to the charity appeals that run weekly on BBC Radio 4. Most begin with a vivid description of how their charity has managed to turn around the life on an individual person.

The small size of your charity is likely to mean that the services you provide are of a small and personal nature, so examples should be easy to find. Anecdotes that focus of specific activities will help illustrate why your charity is worth supporting.

Remember that those helped by your charity may be recognisable to some of your listeners. Think carefully about how to make any example personal without breaching anyone's confidentiality. This may mean changing the story to disguise a person and/or a circumstance or using an example of your charity work that is not too close to the homes of the listeners.

Remember to adopt a tone of speech that is personal and so fits with your content. The phrase 'speaking from the heart' suggests a typical style and tone of the speech that is likely to be more successful.

Does your audience know enough about your charity?
Once you have your audience's attention and have touched their hearts, you will need to convince their minds.

Consider what they already know about your charity. Your charity group may be unknown to some or all of the listeners. If so, your speech will need to establish the credibility of your charity but be careful because too many facts will lose people's attention.

Think about how your charity fits in to a bigger picture and how it is connected to local/national/international issues. For example, although your local charity may be small, it may have support of a much larger organisation or recognition by a large charity agency that the listeners recognise.

Alternatively there may be a prominent person who is supporting your speech and whose judgement the listeners trust. Briefly outlining how your charity fits in will reassure your listeners that donations will be used to support worthwhile charity work and the use of the funds will be scrutinised by a trustworthy organisation or trustworthy individuals.

Bang for your buck or good value
A small charity will usually rely on volunteers who give time freely and therefore overheads will be small. Make this clear so your listeners will know that they will be getting good value for their donations. A common criticism of bigger charities is that their overheads can consume a high proportion of the funds donated.

What other work do you want your audience to know about and support?
Your opening anecdote will have given your listeners a sample but there may be many other examples of needs dealt with by your charity. More examples should broaden your charity's appeal and your listeners. Give you listeners examples of specific works your charity has done, who was helped (remember confidentiality though), when they were helped, how you helped and what change your help made in their lives.

Your charity work is probably not all about money so make this clear. Consider asking your listeners if they would be willing to get involved? The odds are that giving you donations will seem an easier option for them but you never know. If they are short on time, as many people are in our modern society, they may feel more able to donate their money.

Now finish with what you have come to ask
Your audience is expecting you to ask for money, so while you will want to be polite you do not need to feel too self-conscious. If you have known many of them for years, then speak to them as if talking to a friend. If it is a church group, then you can ask them to keep you in their thoughts and prayers. If it is a group of work or business associates, suggest that a small amount from them will mean a great deal to someone less fortunate. Then your final line should be a call to arms, by helping you in a small way they really will make a big difference to other people's lives.

Remember practice and polish
Ask someone to proof-read your speech to pick up things that you unconsciously miss and to give you more insight into the thoughts your speech will conjure up. Ask them if they have any questions about your charity and to be honest about any doubts they have or they think others might have regarding donating. Revise your speech to address these questions and doubts but keep it as simply as possible.

Make sure you have plenty of time to practice your speech and work out any problems. The more time you have to practice, the less likely you will need to read directly from your written speech. If you have time, consider using cue-cards instead and practice until your speech flows easily from one card to the next. Remember that the more natural that your speech sounds to your listeners, the more empathy you are likely to receive towards your cause.

An example speech

Below is an example of a speech that might be given to a church group. The setting is a speaker who may have a microphone but no other audio-visual aids.

This is fictitious but it will hopefully feel real. The spoken tone would ideally be warm and the speech reasonably informal, for example I have used "I'd like" instead of "I would like" in the main body of the speech. The introduction, the short gap for positioning and the speech would take a little under ten minutes all together.

Introductory blurb for the person ("Peter") leading the meeting that I ("John") am addressing (note that this is written more formally).

I would like to introduce John Brown who is a volunteer with our local council of the St Agnes Charity. John's group has provided help for many of our local people in their time of need and he has come today to ask for your help. Please give him a few minutes of your attention.

Peter's speech

Hello everyone. Thank you all for listening and thank you Peter for giving me the opportunity to speak here today. Some of you know about our work already but for those who do not, I would like to describe our work by telling you a little story about Alice.

I met Alice two months after I volunteered to be a member of the St Agnes Charity. Alice lives a few blocks from here but it is unlikely you have ever met her. She's eighty-three years old and has lived in the area for almost her entire life. When she was younger she worked as a home-helper, up until the time she retired. She never had children and it is been many years since her husband, her brother and her sister passed away. Our town has changed a great deal since that time and whilst she remembers the old town, she is also happy to see so many younger families here now.

Alice lives in a house owned by the council and, because she is not very mobile any more, she spends most of her time looking out the window.

The barber on the corner, the local shop keeper and the doctor know her but not well because she does not go out much and lives very simply. Just before I met her, her mobility worsened and she was having trouble doing her shopping. She got desperate and contacted her sister-in-law, Joyce, who lives four hundred miles away. Joyce had remarried when Alice's brother died and her second husband, also in his eighties, was very dependent on her. Joyce was desperately worried but felt unable to help, so she rang one of our local churches and was referred to us.

Within a couple of days we had visited Alice and were astounded by her situation. Although she was renting a home from the council, no-one had done any maintenance for decades. There was no hot water: the boiler was broken and looked at least forty years old. The only source of heat was a gas heater in the living room, itself at least twenty years old but working well, and the only water was from the cold tap in the kitchen.

Furthermore, Alice had been unable to get into the deep old bath for many years, so she washed herself with a flannel and a bowl of water, partly filled by her kettle. She flushed her upstairs toilet with water carried from the kitchen downstairs and she could not remember how long she had needed to do that. Her memory was not so good anymore.
None of Alice's windows opened apart from her bedroom window, which was stuck open making it far too cold to sleep in there. Her legs were swollen from sleeping in her chair, so it was no wonder she could not get about very well anymore.

She was most worried about whether her rent needed paying because she hadn't been able to get to the post office to pay it and she had lost her rent book. Apart from that she did not seem concerned by her living situation. We did a bit of shopping and prepared her a meal. She was obviously quite hungry. She hadn't been able to get to the bank and was living on packets of mash potato and cups of tea. She was so grateful that we had come to help but she really did not want to bother us.

We've known Alice for about a year now. She hasn't allowed us to do too much but she is so grateful for even the small things we do. We organised regular home help and eventually got the council to put in a new boiler, central heating, and a new bathroom suite and get the water flowing around the house.

Alice still cannot use the bath but the occupational therapist recommended assistance rather than a shower with a seat. Alice still wants to be independent and does not realise how much help she needs.

The best thing we have done for Alice is show her that someone cares. Her face lights up whenever one of us sits down in her living room and she tells the same old story about when she fell in the snow.

She does not remember most of the times when we go to the bank or when we stop for lunch afterwards, but she remembers enough to know that we do it sometimes and I think she loves us for it. It is a real treat for us too. It feels so good to bring happiness into her simple life.

We visit many other people in our community and help them however we can. Sometimes we will just keep someone company for a little while. Sometimes we provide household items such as second hand wardrobes or maybe a new bed. Sometimes we help them repair what they already have. Sometimes we give them money towards specific needs, such as a carpet to cover the draughty floorboards, or help a child fund a school trip.

There seem to be so many people, even in our local area, who are ignored by society. We wish we could do more but most of us have our full time jobs or families to look after full-time and our resources are limited. If you could spare a couple of hours a week, we would love to hear from you. Please come and speak to me later. If you cannot spare any time, then perhaps you could spare some money to help our work along.

We are a small charity with few overheads. We meet in the church hall, which is provided freely by the local parish, and we do not need much else to run the local group. But we do need money to help people like Alice out from time to time and you can be sure that your donations will make a real difference to real people.

We'll be passing around some envelopes, so please give what you can. If you pay tax, you can fill in some details so these donations will be recognised by the tax office. Our contact details are also there if you decide later you could help by joining our group.

If you do not feel able to help in these ways then please do bear us in mind for the future. Thank you again for your time and for listening.

Some things to note

- The speech above is probably at the upper limit of length.

- The story was designed to get their attention and grab their hearts.

- The credibility of the charity was established by the connections with the person introducing the speaker, the introductory blurb, the suggestion that some of the listeners were already familiar with the charity work and also the connections with the local church that saw fit to lend their venue to the charity group.

- The "bang for your buck" was established by references to volunteers and low overheads.

- The story was followed by a quick reference to other works. Facts and figures were avoided.

- The tone of the writing was casual and designed to be spoken from the heart.